INTRODUCTION

Knowing that you look good – that a pair of pants or a blouse is cut just right, that a skirt trims your figure, that a piece of jewelry accents your outfit perfectly – can give you a feeling of supreme confidence. Fashion icons like Audrey Hepburn, Grace Kelly, and Jaqueline Kennedy Onassis seemed to have a natural talent for finding such chic ensembles. For the average woman, though, it can sometimes seem impossible to find the time or the know-how to pull together an outfit that both flatters and expresses a personal style.

Learning how to use clothing and accessories to their full advantage is half the battle. Just as you wouldn't expect even a beautifully made dress to complement your figure if it was in the wrong size, jewelry won't help you look your best unless it is chosen based on face shape and clothing lines.

That's where *Jewelry Just for You! Projects That Flatter Every Face Shape and Neckline* comes in. Unsure what will best flatter your oval face? Want to make a necklace that will stun with a strapless dress? The projects in this book are organized in two sections, the first divided by face shape, and the second divided by neckline. Two versatile pieces, one that can be adapted for any face shape and one that can be adjusted for any neckline, are also included. Armed with the knowledge that your chin-length earrings, like those in Molli Schultz's article, "Try angular" (p. 27), are perfect for your heart-shaped face, or that the choker from Sara Strauss's "Circle of Light" (p. 58) is just right for the round neckline of your shirt, you can head out – whether it's to the opera or just to pick the kids up after school – with all the confidence of a fashion icon.

round face heart-shaped face oval face squa

-neck strapless round neckline turtleneck v-

JEWELRY JUST FOR YOU!

p. 12

p. 27

Face shapes PAGE 8

p. 36

JEWELRY JUST FOR YOU!

Projects that flatter
every face shape
and neckline

Printed in the United States of America.

12 11 10 09 08 1 2 3 4 5

Publisher's Cataloging-In-Publication Data
(Prepared by The Donohue Group, Inc.)

Jewelry just for you! : projects that flatter every face shape and neckline.

   p. : col. ill. ; cm.

   Material previously published in BeadStyle magazine special issue, Your perfect look.
   ISBN: 978-0-87116-261-8

1. Beadwork--Handbooks, manuals, etc. 2. Beadwork--patterns. 3. Jewelry making--Handbooks, manuals, etc. 4. Dress accessories. I. Title: BeadStyle Magazine

TT860 .J49 2008
745.594/2

p. 81

p. 78

p. 34

Necklines PAGE 50

p. 61

BASICS

LOOPS AND JUMP RINGS

Plain loop

1 Trim the wire or head pin ⅜ in. (1cm) above the top bead. Make a right-angle bend close to the bead.

2 Grab the wire's tip with roundnose pliers. The tip of the wire should be flush with the pliers. Roll the wire to form a half circle. Release the wire.

3 Reposition the pliers in the loop and continue rolling.

4 The finished loop should form a centered circle above the bead.

Wrapped loop

1 Make sure you have at least 1¼ in. (3.2cm) of wire above the bead. With the tip of your chainnose pliers, grasp the wire directly above the bead. Bend the wire (above the pliers) into a right angle.

3 Bring the wire over the top jaw of the roundnose pliers.

5 Position the chainnose pliers' jaws across the loop.

2 Position the jaws of a pair of roundnose pliers in the bend.

4 Reposition the pliers' lower jaw snugly into the loop. Curve the wire downward around the bottom of the roundnose pliers. This is the first half of a wrapped loop.

6 Wrap the wire around the wire stem, covering the stem between the loop and the top bead. Trim the excess wire and press the cut end close to the wraps with chainnose pliers.

Make a set of wraps above a top-drilled bead

1 Center a top-drilled bead on a 3-in. (7.6cm) piece of wire. Bend each wire upward to form a squared-off "U" shape.

2 Cross the wires into an "X" above the bead.

3 Using chainnose pliers, make a small bend in each wire so the ends form a right angle.

4 Wrap the horizontal wire around the vertical wire as in a wrapped loop. Trim the excess wire.

Open a split ring

Slide the hooked tip of split-ring pliers between the two overlapping wires.

Open and close loops or jump rings

1 Hold the loop or jump ring with two pairs of chainnose pliers or chainnose and roundnose pliers, as shown.

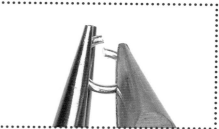

2 To open the loop or jump ring, bring one pair of pliers toward you and push the other pair away. String materials on the open loop or jump ring. Reverse the steps to close the open loop or jump ring.

CRIMPS

Folded end crimp

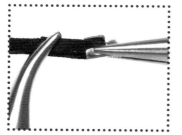

1 Glue one end of the cord and place it in a crimp end. Use chainnose pliers to fold one side of the crimp end over the cord.

2 Repeat with the second side of the crimp end and squeeze gently.

Folded crimp

1 Position the crimp bead in the notch closest to the crimping pliers' handle.

2 Separate the wires and firmly squeeze the crimp.

Flattened crimp

1 Hold the crimp using the tip of your chainnose pliers. Squeeze the pliers firmly to flatten the crimp.

2 Tug the wire to make sure the crimp has a solid grip. If the wire slides, repeat the steps with a new crimp.

3 Move the crimp into the notch at the pliers' tip and hold the crimp as shown. Squeeze the crimp bead, folding it in half at the indentation.

4 Test that the folded crimp is secure.

Face shapes

1
Round
PAGE 10

With a circular shape and full cheeks, a round face looks best with jewelry that creates a slimming effect. Wear longer necklaces to create the illusion of facial length, or pieces with a focal point that draws the eye down. For earrings, look for square or rectangle shapes and long dangles that draw attention downward.

2
Square
PAGE 18

With clearly defined angles, a square face looks best with jewelry that adds curves. A strong, wide chin looks balanced when a necklace's focal point draws the eye downward. Curvy earrings soften the angles as well.

3
Heart
PAGE 27

Wider at the forehead and narrower at the chin, a heart-shaped face is well served by jewelry that gives the illusion of width to the jawline, such as necklaces with strong horizontal lines or chunky beads. Earrings that move the eye from side to side, especially at chin level, are also very flattering.

4
Oval
PAGE 36

With well-proportioned features, an oval face often is considered the ideal face shape for design purposes. Since any type of necklace or earrings will work, take advantage of the freedom to experiment. Play with unexpected combinations of shapes and textures.

All face shapes
PAGE 46

Try our "Versatile crystals" project that can be adjusted to complement any face shape.

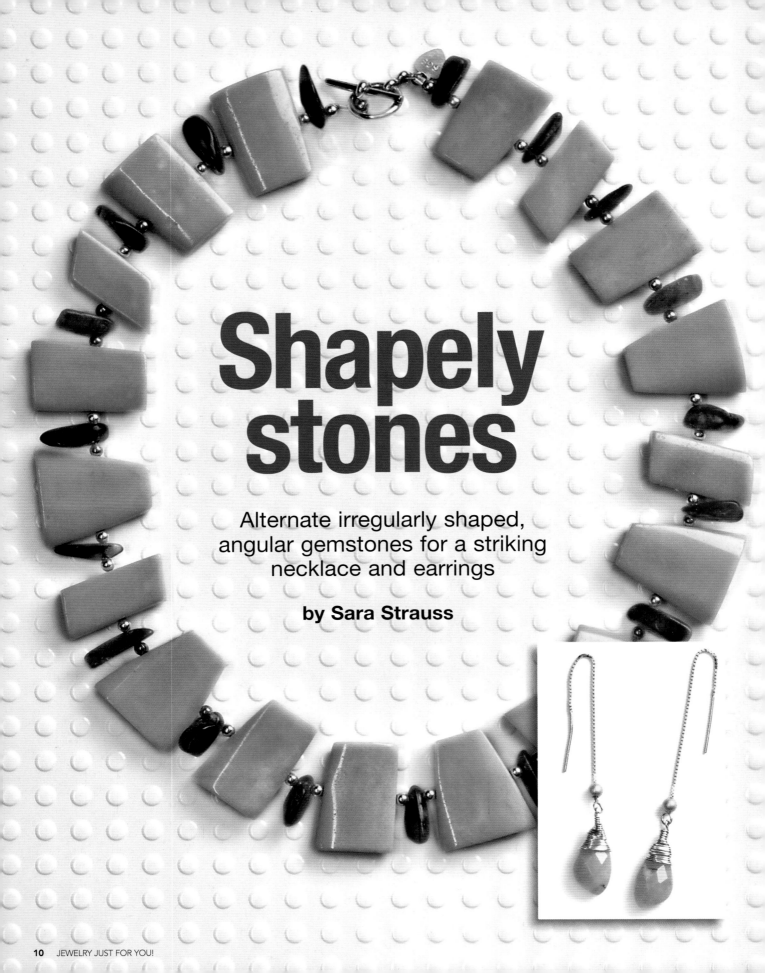

Shapely stones

Alternate irregularly shaped, angular gemstones for a striking necklace and earrings

by Sara Strauss

Although this necklace and these earrings take but a moment to string, the success of this striking set comes from the planning. Before stringing, lay out your gemstones. Set aside two matching drops for the earrings. Then, center the largest stones, and position smaller stones on each end. Be mindful of color combinations when designing this optimally balanced set.

1 **necklace** • Determine the finished length of your necklace. (These necklaces are 15½ in./ 39.4cm.) Add 6 in. (15cm) and cut a piece of beading wire to that length. Center a drop bead.

2 On each end, string a spacer, an irregular slab, and a spacer.

3 On each end, string a drop, a spacer, a slab, and a spacer. Repeat until the strand is within 2 in. (5cm) of the desired length. End with a spacer.

4 On each end, string a drop, a spacer, a crimp bead, a spacer, and half of a clasp. Go back through the last three beads strung and tighten the wire. Check the fit, and add or remove beads from each end if necessary. Crimp the crimp beads (Basics, p. 6) and trim the excess wire.

EDITOR'S TIP
Use irregular gemstone slabs. Their angles will flatter a round face.

1 **earrings** • Cut a 10-in. (25cm) piece of wire. String a drop bead 1½ in. (3.8cm) from one end. Bend each wire upward to form an X above the bead. Using chainnose pliers, bend each wire to form a right angle, with the short end vertical and the long end horizontal.

3 Wrap the horizontal wire around the top of the drop.
   Open the loop of an earring thread and attach the dangle. Close the loop. If desired, string a spacer on the earring thread. Make a second earring to match the first.

2 Make a wrapped loop (Basics) with the vertical wire.

SUPPLY LIST

necklace
• 16-in. (41cm) strand gemstone slabs, horizontally drilled
• 16-in. (41cm) strand gemstone drops, top drilled
• **40–44** 3–4mm round spacers
• flexible beading wire, .014 or .015
• **2** crimp beads
• clasp
• chainnose or crimping pliers
• diagonal wire cutters

earrings
• **2** gemstone drops, top drilled
• **2** 3–4mm spacers (optional)
• 20 in. (51cm) 24-gauge half-hard wire
• pair of earring threads
• chainnose pliers
• roundnose pliers
• diagonal wire cutters

Arrange drops and ovals in a
staggered pattern to offset your curves

Dropping hints

by Jennifer Gorski

Faceted oval beads and drops placed at staggered
lengths converge in a long pendant. The effect: the
angles draw the eye downward. For variety, make
different versions — one in bright, contrasting colors
and one in muted tones. Dangly earrings gracefully
reflect the theme.

SUPPLY LIST

necklace
- 20 x 40mm drop pendant
  with bail or jump ring
- **10–12** faceted oval beads,
  approximately 8 x 12mm
- **6** 8 x 10mm briolettes
- **14–16** 5mm round pearls
- **34–38** 4mm bicone
  crystals
- **16–20** 3mm round crystals

- **3–5** 11º seed beads
  (optional)
- flexible beading wire,
  .014 or .015
- 6 in. (15cm) 24-gauge
  half-hard wire
- **2** crimp beads
- clasp
- chainnose pliers
- roundnose pliers
- diagonal wire cutters
- crimping pliers (optional)

earrings
- **2** faceted oval beads,
  approximately 8 x 12mm
- **2** 8 x 10mm briolettes
- **2** 5mm round pearls
- **2** 4mm bicone crystals
- 11 in. (28cm) 24-gauge
  half-hard wire
- pair of earring wires
- chainnose pliers
- roundnose pliers
- diagonal wire cutters

1 **necklace** • Cut a 3-in. (7.6cm) piece of 24-gauge wire. String a briolette and make a set of wraps above it (Basics, p. 6). String a bicone crystal and make a wrapped loop (Basics) perpendicular to the briolette. Make a second dangle.

2 Determine the finished length of your necklace. (These necklaces are 15 in./38cm.) Add 6 in. (15cm) and cut a piece of beading wire to that length. If the pendant has a bail (rather than a jump ring), string three to five 11º seed beads. Center the pendant on the wire so it rests on the 11ºs.

3 On each end, string a bicone, an oval bead, a bicone, and a dangle.

4 On each end, string a bicone, a pearl, a bicone, and a briolette. Repeat.

5 On each end, string a bicone, a pearl, a bicone, and an oval. Repeat the pattern until the necklace is within 3 in. (7.6cm) of the desired length.

6 On each end, string seven 3mm crystals, a crimp bead, a 3mm crystal, and half of a clasp. Go back through the last three beads strung and tighten the wire. Check the fit, and add or remove beads from each end if necessary. Crimp the crimp beads (Basics) and trim the excess wire.

1 **earrings** • Cut a 3-in. (7.6cm) piece of 24-gauge wire. String a briolette and make a set of wraps above it (Basics). String a pearl and a bicone crystal and make the first half of a wrapped loop (Basics) perpendicular to the briolette.

2 Cut a 2½-in. (6.4cm) piece of wire. Make the first half of a wrapped loop on one end. String an oval bead and make the first half of a wrapped loop above the bead.

3 Attach the briolette unit to a loop of the oval unit. Complete the wraps.

4 Open the loop (Basics) of an earring wire, attach the dangle, and close the loop. Make a second earring to match the first.

Vermeil squares grace
this textured necklace
with a soft glow

by Cathy Jakicic

Angles are
among us as the
curves of crystals
and pearls balance
boxy ceramic and
vermeil elements.
Four-hole squares
allow you to turn a
stylish corner, while the
length of the strand
balances round
facial contours.

Believe in

1 necklace • Determine the finished length of your necklace. (This one is 30 in./76cm.) Add 6 in. (15cm) and cut a piece of beading wire to that length. On the wire, center: two pearls, square ceramic bead, two pearls, crystal, two pearls, ceramic bead, two pearls.

2 On each end, string one hole of the four-hole square bead, two crystals, and an adjacent hole of the four-hole square bead.

3 On each end, string two pearls, a crystal, two pearls, and a ceramic bead. Repeat until the necklace is within 1½ in. (3.8cm) of the desired length.

4 On one end, string a spacer, a crimp bead, a spacer, and a lobster claw clasp. Go back through the last four beads strung and tighten the wire. Repeat on the other end, substituting a soldered jump ring for the clasp. Check the fit, and add or remove beads from each end if necessary. Crimp the crimp beads (Basics, p. 6) and trim the excess wire.

SUPPLY LIST

necklace
- **16–18** 18mm square ceramic beads (JP Imported, 707-541-0301)
- **2** four-hole square vermeil beads (The Bead Shop, 650-328-5291, beadshop.com)
- **16**-in. (41cm) strand 6mm button pearls
- **19–23** 4mm cube crystals, diagonally drilled
- **4** 4mm spacers
- flexible beading wire, .014 or .015
- **2** crimp beads
- lobster claw clasp and soldered jump ring

- chainnose or crimping pliers
- diagonal wire cutters

earrings
- **2** 18mm square ceramic beads (JP Imported)
- **2** four-hole square vermeil beads (The Bead Shop)
- **2** 6mm button pearls
- **4** 4mm cube crystals, diagonally drilled
- **2** 4mm spacers
- **2** 3-in. (7.6cm) head pins
- pair of earring wires
- chainnose pliers
- roundnose pliers
- diagonal wire cutters

1 earrings • On a head pin, string: pearl, bottom hole of a four-hole square bead, crystal, spacer, crystal, top hole of the four-hole square bead, square ceramic bead. Make a plain loop (Basics) above the ceramic bead.

2 Open the loop (Basics) of an earring wire and attach the dangle. Close the loop. Make a second earring to match the first.

angles

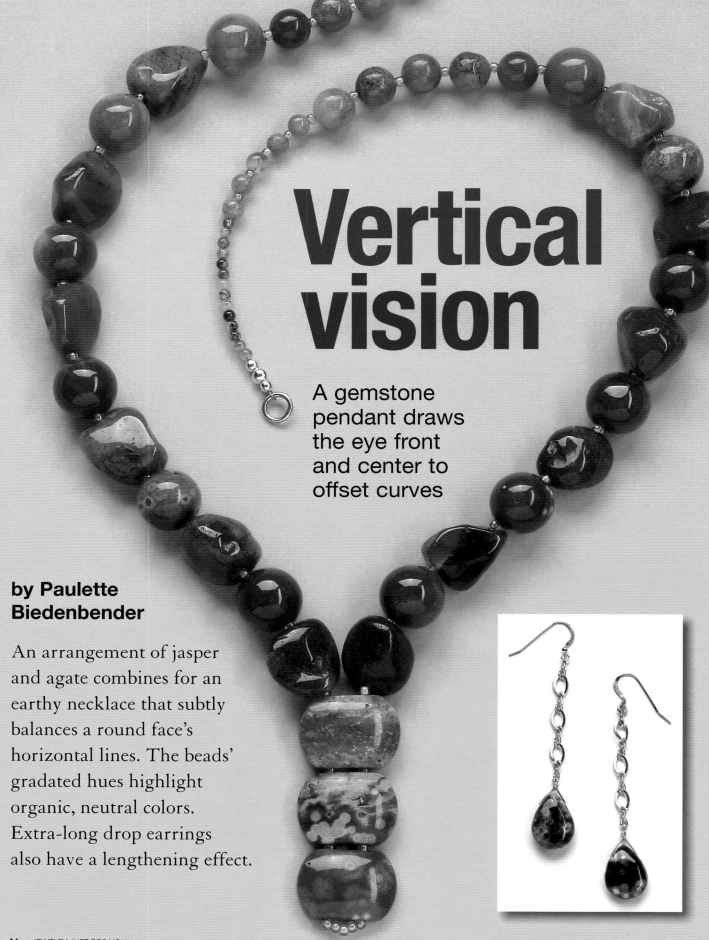

Vertical vision

A gemstone pendant draws the eye front and center to offset curves

by Paulette Biedenbender

An arrangement of jasper and agate combines for an earthy necklace that subtly balances a round face's horizontal lines. The beads' gradated hues highlight organic, neutral colors. Extra-long drop earrings also have a lengthening effect.

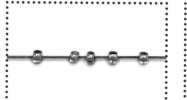

1 **necklace** • Determine the finished length of your necklace. (This one is 27 in./69cm.) Add 6 in. (15cm) and cut a piece of beading wire to that length. Center five 11º seed beads on the wire.

2 String a two-hole bead over both ends. String an 11º on each end. Repeat twice.

3 On each end, string a nugget, an 11º, a 10mm round bead, and an 11º. Repeat for 5–6 in. (13–15cm). End with a 10mm and an 11º.

1 **earrings** • Cut a 4-in. (10cm) piece of wire. String a teardrop bead. Make a set of wraps above the bead (Basics). Make a plain loop (Basics) above the wraps, perpendicular to the bead.

4 On each end, string a 6mm round bead and an 11º. Repeat for 1–2 in. (2.5–5cm). End with an 11º.

5 On each end, string a 4mm round bead and an 11º. Repeat for ½–1 in. (1.3–2.5cm). End with a 4mm.

6 String 2mm round beads until the necklace is within 1 in. (2.5cm) of the desired length.

7 On each end, string a spacer, a crimp bead, a spacer, and a soldered jump ring. Go back through the beads just strung and tighten the wires. Check the fit, and add or remove beads from each end if necessary. Crimp the crimp beads (Basics, p. 6). Use chainnose pliers to attach an S-hook clasp to one of the jump rings. If desired, close a crimp cover over each crimp bead.

2 Cut a 2-in. (5cm) piece of chain. Open the loop of the bead unit and attach it to the chain. Close the loop.

3 Open the loop (Basics) of an earring wire and attach the dangle. Close the loop. Make a second earring to match the first.

SUPPLY LIST

necklace
- **3** 15 x 20mm two-hole rectangle beads
- 16-in. (41cm) strand 13mm nuggets
- 16-in. (41cm) strand 10mm round beads
- 16-in. (41cm) strand 2mm round beads
- **10–14** 6mm round beads
- **10–14** 4mm round beads
- 1g 11º seed beads
- **4** 2mm round spacers
- flexible beading wire, .014 or .015
- **2** crimp beads
- **2** crimp covers (optional)
- S-hook clasp and **2** soldered jump rings
- chainnose pliers
- diagonal wire cutters
- crimping pliers (optional)

earrings
- **2** 15 x 20mm teardrop beads, top drilled
- 8 in. (20cm) 24-gauge half-hard wire
- 5 in. (13cm) large-and-small-link chain, 6–7mm links
- pair of earring wires
- chainnose pliers
- roundnose pliers
- diagonal wire cutters

EDITOR'S TIP
Before stringing, group the beads by color and arrange them from dark to light. The necklace will show a wider range of color tones.

Round
the corners

Circular beads and extra length soften the angles

by Cathy Jakicic

Long lines and bold colors draw the eye to the round beads and resin disks that will help you turn the corner in balancing a square face. Keeping the matching earrings short and away from a strong jawline will also let you find the softer side of square.

1 necklace • Determine the finished length of your necklace. (This one is 24 in./ 61cm.) Add 6 in. (15cm) and cut a piece of beading wire to that length. On the wire, center: resin round bead, 6mm round bead, resin coin bead, 6mm round, pendant, 6mm round, coin, 6mm round, resin round.

2 On each end, string a 6mm round and a coin. Repeat until the necklace is within 1 in. (2.5cm) of the desired length. End with a coin.

3 On one end, string a 6mm round, a crimp bead, a 6mm round, and a lobster claw clasp. Go back through the beads just strung and tighten the wire. Repeat on the other end, substituting a soldered jump ring for the clasp. Check the fit, and add or remove an equal number of beads from each end if necessary. Crimp the crimp beads (Basics, p. 6) and trim the excess wire.

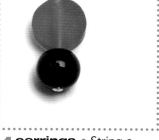

1 earrings • String a 6mm round bead and a coin bead on a head pin. Make the first half of a wrapped loop (Basics) above the coin.

2 Attach the dangle to the loop of an earring post. Complete the wraps. Make a second earring to match the first.

EDITOR'S TIP Select round beads with a shiny finish to contrast with the matte finish of the resin beads.

SUPPLY LIST

necklace
- triangular resin pendant (all resin beads from Natural Touch Beads, 707-781-0808, naturaltouchbeads.com)
- **2** 21mm resin round beads
- 16-in. (41cm) strand 8mm resin coin beads
- 16-in. (41cm) strand 6mm round beads
- flexible beading wire, .014 or .015
- **2** crimp beads
- lobster claw clasp and soldered jump ring
- chainnose or crimping pliers
- diagonal wire cutters

earrings
- **2** 8mm resin coin beads (Natural Touch Beads)
- **2** 6mm round beads
- **2** 3-in. (7.6cm) head pins
- pair of earring posts with ear nuts
- chainnose pliers
- roundnose pliers
- diagonal wire cutters

The long way

An easy beaded necklace and lean earrings add drama to any outfit

by Naomi Fujimoto

Simplicity dazzles in this necklace of gumball-sized round beads. For a graduated look, string beads in three sizes. Consider Lucite or wood as design options — they're lightweight and available in many sizes. Don't forget the earrings: like the necklace, they draw the eye downward.

1 **necklace •** Determine the finished length of your necklace. (This one is 34 in./86cm.) Add 6 in. (15cm), and cut two pieces of beading wire to that length. Center a 20mm round bead over both wires. On each end, string a spacer and a 20mm round, repeating until the necklace is half the desired length. End with a spacer.

2 On each end, string an 18mm round bead and a spacer, repeating until the necklace is within 3 in. (7.6cm) of the desired length. End with a spacer.

3 On each end, string: 12mm round bead, crimp bead, 12mm round, spacer, 12mm round. On one end, string a spacer.

4 String each pair of wires through the beads just strung on the opposite side. Tighten the wires. Check the fit, and add or remove beads from each end if necessary. Crimp the crimp beads (Basics, p. 6) and trim the excess wire.

EDITOR'S TIP
If desired, finish the necklace with 18mm, rather than 12mm, round beads. However, the 12mm round beads create less bulk at the back of the necklace.

1 **earrings •** On a head pin, string a 12mm round bead, a pearl, and a spacer. Make a plain loop (Basics) above the spacer.

2 Cut a 1-in. (2.5cm) piece of chain. Open the bead unit's loop (Basics) and attach the chain. Close the loop.

3 Open the loop of an earring wire. Attach the dangle and close the loop. Make a second earring to match the first.

SUPPLY LIST

necklace
- 16-in. (41cm) strand 20mm round beads
- 16-in. (41cm) strand 18mm round beads
- **6–10** 12–15mm round beads
- **40–50** 4mm flat spacers
- flexible beading wire, .018 or .019
- **2** crimp beads
- chainnose or crimping pliers
- diagonal wire cutters

earrings
- **2** 12–15mm round beads
- **2** 8–12mm round pearls
- **2** 4mm flat spacers
- 2 in. (5cm) cable chain, 2–3mm links
- **2** 1½-in. (3.8cm) 22-gauge head pins
- pair of earring wires
- chainnose pliers
- roundnose pliers
- diagonal wire cutters

Transform a shapely
pendant and swirls of chain
into a stunning necklace

Scalloped curves

by Gloria Farver

SUPPLY LIST

necklace
- 35–40mm triangle pendant, side drilled
- **7–9** 9mm teardrop beads
- **7–9** 5mm rondelles
- **7–9** 4–6mm round beads
- **18–22** 4mm bicone crystals
- **34–42** 3mm bicone crystals
- 2g 11º seed beads

- flexible beading wire, .014 or .015
- 22–26 in. (56–66cm) cable chain, 2mm links
- 1 in. (2.5cm) cable chain, 5mm links
- **3** 1½-in. (3.8cm) head pins
- 5mm jump ring
- **2** crimp beads

- toggle clasp
- chainnose pliers
- roundnose pliers
- diagonal wire cutters
- crimping pliers (optional)

earrings
- **2** 9mm teardrop beads
- **2** 9mm rondelles
- **4** 3mm bicone crystals

- **2** 5mm spacers
- 2 in. (5cm) 20-gauge half-hard wire
- **2** 1½-in. (3.8cm) 26-gauge decorative head pins
- pair of earring wires
- chainnose pliers
- roundnose pliers
- diagonal wire cutters

Loosely strung chain and a smooth jasper pendant create soft edges that flatter a square face. Don't skimp on the details — dangles at the nape of the neck and trouble-free earrings are the finishing touches.

1 **necklace** • To make a bead unit, string an 11º seed bead, a 3mm bicone crystal, a rondelle, a 3mm bicone, and an 11º on a head pin. Make the first half of a wrapped loop (Basics, p. 6) above the 11º. Make two more bead units, substituting a teardrop bead and then a round bead for the rondelle.

2 Cut a 1-in. (2.5cm) piece of 5mm chain. On one end, attach each bead unit and complete the wraps. On the other end, open a jump ring (Basics) and attach the bar half of a toggle clasp. Close the jump ring. Set aside for step 7.

3 **a** Determine the finished length of your necklace. (This one is 16 in./ 41cm.) Add 6 in. (15cm) and cut a piece of beading wire and a piece of 2mm chain to that length. Cut the chain in half. Center the pendant on the wire.

b On each side, string a 4mm bicone crystal and three 11ºs.

4 On each side, string: 2mm chain link, 4mm bicone, three 11ºs, 3mm bicone, rondelle, 3mm bicone, three 11ºs, chain link.

5 Repeat step 4, substituting a teardrop for the rondelle.

6 **a** Repeat step 4, substituting a round for the rondelle.

b Repeat steps 5, 4, 6a, and 4 until the strand is within 1 in. (2.5cm) of the desired length. End with a 4mm bicone. Trim the excess chain.

7 On each end, string an 11º, a crimp bead, 10 11ºs, and half of the clasp. Go back through the first 11º, a crimp bead, an 11º, and a bicone. Tighten the wire, check the fit, and add or remove beads from each end if necessary. Crimp the crimp beads (Basics) and trim the excess wire.

EDITOR'S TIP To give your necklace a more formal look, choose a pendant, seed beads, and crystals in a monochromatic palette.

1 **earrings** • On a decorative head pin, string: bicone crystal, teardrop bead, spacer, bicone. Make a wrapped loop (Basics) above the top bead.

2 Cut a 1-in. (2.5cm) piece of wire. Make a plain loop (Basics) on one end. String a rondelle and make a plain loop above the bead.

3 Open a loop (Basics) of the rondelle unit and attach the wrapped-loop unit. Close the loop.

4 Open an earring wire and attach the dangle. Close the wire. Make a second earring to match the first.

Flow
motion

Tiny faceted rondelles shimmer in angle-softening waves

by Naomi Fujimoto

The subtle flow of this multistrand necklace has a gentling influence on an angular face. Mostly monochromatic, the necklace's fluid lines get tiny punches of color from sapphires and gold spacers. Make this piece with garnets or substitute Czech glass, but stay with the short length and small, faceted rondelles to maintain its subtlety and the face-framing scale.

1 necklace • Determine the finished length of your necklace. (This one is 15½ in./39.4cm.) Add 8 in. (20cm) and cut 12 pieces of beading wire to that length. On four wires, string main-color rondelles until each strand is within 2 in. (5cm) of the desired length.

2 On one wire, center 12 main rondelles. On each end, string an accent-color rondelle, a flat spacer, and an accent rondelle. Alternate the main and accent patterns, repeating until the strand is within 2 in. (5cm) of the desired length.

3 On one wire, center an accent rondelle, a flat spacer, and an accent rondelle. On each end, string 14 main rondelles. Alternate the accent and main patterns, repeating until the strand is within 2 in. (5cm) of the desired length.

4 String a main pattern and an accent pattern on the remaining wires, each with two more rondelles in the main pattern than the previous strand. Repeat until each strand is within 2 in. (5cm) of the desired length. (The remaining strands in this necklace have main patterns with 16, 18, 20, 22, 24, and 26 rondelles.) For balance, string some strands with main patterns at the center and some with accent patterns.

5 Check the fit of each strand, allowing 2 in. (5cm) for finishing. Add or remove beads from each end if necessary. Tie a knot on each end of each strand. Do not trim the excess beading wire.

Cut six 4-in. (10cm) pieces of 24-gauge wire. Make a 3mm wrapped loop (Basics, p. 6) at one end of each wire.

6 Group the 12 strands into three sets of four, putting at least one main-color strand in each set. For each set: On each side, over all four wires, string a large-hole bead, a crimp bead, and the wrapped loop. Go back through the beads just strung and tighten the wires. Crimp the crimp beads (Basics) and trim the excess beading wire.

EDITOR'S TIPS

• When taping one end of a wire, label it with the number of main-color rondelles strung in each pattern so you can quickly identify each strand's pattern — it's handy if you're stringing the strands in different sessions.

• It is difficult to make each strand the perfect length in relation to the others. The chain extender builds in flexibility to make the necklace drape beautifully.

7 Gather the three sets together. Over all three wires, string a beading cone and a large-hole bead. Make a wrapped loop with all three wires. Repeat on the other side.

8 Open a jump ring (Basics). On one end, attach a wrapped loop and a lobster claw clasp. Close the jump ring. Repeat on the other end, substituting a 2½-in. (6.4cm) piece of chain for the clasp.

9 String a rondelle and a large-hole bead on a head pin. Make the first half of a wrapped loop. Attach it to the chain and complete the wraps.

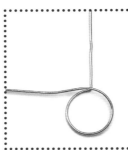

1 **earrings** • String a rondelle on a head pin. Make a wrapped loop (Basics) above the bead. Make a total of five bead units.

2 Cut a 3½-in. (8.9cm) piece of wire. Wrap it around a round object with a ⅜-in. (1cm) diameter. Remove the object. Make an upward right-angle bend where the wires cross.

3 String the bead units on the loop. Wrap the horizontal wire around the vertical wire, completing the wraps. Make a plain or wrapped loop (Basics) with the vertical wire.

4 Open the loop (Basics) of an earring wire and attach the dangle. Make a second earring the mirror image of the first.

by Molli Schultz

Try angular

String crystals and filigree beads in a sparkling necklace and geometric earrings

For jewelry that looks both contemporary and vintage, crystals and filigree are a natural pairing. The necklace's strung section creates a horizontal line, while triangular earrings visually extend the line, balancing a narrow chin. Try making multiple sets — consider using silver filigree with black or gray crystals.

EDITOR'S TIP
If you prefer a longer necklace, extend the beaded portion: String additional 6mm filigree beads and crystals on each end.

1 necklace • Cut a 10-in. (25cm) piece of beading wire. String an alternating pattern of six 8mm crystals and five 10mm filigree beads. Center the beads.

2 On each end, string a 6mm filigree bead, a 6mm crystal, a 6mm filigree, and a 6mm crystal.

3 Determine the finished length of your necklace. (This one is 16 in./41cm.) Subtract the length of the beaded section, divide the resulting number in half, and cut two pieces of chain to that length.
On each end of the beaded strand, string a crimp bead and a chain. Go back through the beads just strung, tighten the wires, and crimp the crimp beads (Basics, p. 6).

4 Check the fit, and trim chain from each end if necessary. Open a jump ring (Basics). On one end, attach a lobster claw clasp and the chain. Close the jump ring. Repeat on the other end, substituting a soldered jump ring for the clasp.

1 **earrings** • String a 6mm round crystal on a head pin. Make a plain loop (Basics) above the bead.

2 Cut a ¾-in. (1.9cm) piece of chain. Open the loop of the bead unit and attach the chain. Close the loop. Set aside for step 6.

3 Cut a 3½-in. (8.9cm) piece of wire. Make the first half of a wrapped loop (Basics) at one end. String: bicone crystal, round filigree bead, bicone, filigree tube bead, bicone, round, bicone. Make the first half of a wrapped loop at the other end. Make a total of three long bead units.

4 Attach the loops of one long bead unit to a loop of each of the other two units. Complete the wraps.

5 To make a short bead unit: Cut a 2½-in. (6.4cm) piece of wire. Make the first half of a wrapped loop at one end. String a round, a bicone, and a round. Make the first half of a wrapped loop at the other end.

6 To a loop of the short bead unit, attach the loop of a long bead unit, the chain dangle, and the loop of the remaining long bead unit. Complete the wraps of both loops.

7 Open the loop (Basics) of an earring wire. Attach the dangle and close the loop. Make a second earring to match the first.

SUPPLY LIST

necklace
- **5** 10mm round filigree beads (Shipwreck Beads, 800-950-4232, shipwreckbeads.com)
- **4–6** 6mm round filigree beads (Shipwreck Beads)

- **6** 8mm round crystals
- **4–6** 6mm round crystals
- flexible beading wire, .014 or .015
- 9–11 in. (23–28cm) cable chain, 4–5mm links
- **2** 4mm jump rings
- **2** crimp beads
- lobster claw clasp and soldered jump ring

- chainnose or crimping pliers
- diagonal wire cutters

earrings
- **6** 4 x 8mm filigree tubes (Michaels, michaels.com)
- **16** 4mm round filigree beads (Michaels)
- **2** 6mm round crystals

- **26** 4mm bicone crystals
- 26 in. (66cm) 24-gauge half-hard wire
- 1½ in. (3.8cm) cable or rolo chain, 2–3mm links
- **2** 1-in. (2.5cm) head pins
- pair of earring wires
- chainnose pliers
- roundnose pliers
- diagonal wire cutters

Curve your enthusiasm

Widen a narrow chin with a line of briolettes

by Cathy Jakicic

A curve of multicolored briolettes and liquid silver has wide appeal without overwhelming the delicate features that often accompany a heart-shaped face. Earrings that skim the jawline enhance the illusion of width.

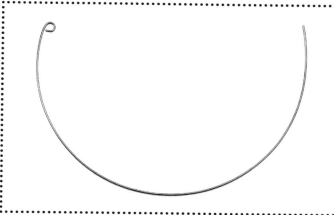

2 String two liquid silver beads and a briolette. Repeat until the beads are within 1 in. (2.5cm) of the wire's end.

String two liquid silver beads and make a loop on the end of the wire, leaving the loop slightly open.

3 Determine the finished length of your necklace. (This one is 18½ in./47cm.) Subtract 3½ in. (8.9cm), divide that number in half, and cut two pieces of chain to that length. Attach a piece of chain to the loop on each end of the briolette strand. Close the loops. Check the fit and trim links from each end if necessary.

1 necklace • Separate 7 in. (18cm) of memory wire from a stack of coils. Hold the wire with chainnose pliers and bend it back and forth at one place until the wire breaks. You also can use heavy-duty wire cutters.

Using roundnose pliers, make a small loop on one end of the memory wire, leaving it slightly open.

4 Open a jump ring (Basics, p. 6). Attach half of a clasp and one chain. Close the jump ring. Repeat on the other end with the other clasp half.

EDITOR'S TIP

Keep the necklace between 14½–18½ in. (36.8–47cm) long. Making it too long will counteract the broadening effect of the line of briolettes.

SUPPLY LIST

necklace
- **8–10** 13 x 18mm briolettes
- **18–22** 5mm twisted liquid-silver beads
- memory wire, necklace diameter
- **11–15 in. (28–38cm)** cable chain, 3mm links
- **2** 4mm jump rings
- clasp
- chainnose pliers
- roundnose pliers
- diagonal wire cutters
- heavy-duty wire cutters (optional)

earrings
- **2** 13 x 18mm briolettes
- **8** 5mm twisted liquid-silver beads
- memory wire, necklace diameter
- **9 in. (23cm)** cable chain, 3mm links
- **2** jump rings
- pair of earring wires
- chainnose pliers
- roundnose pliers
- diagonal wire cutters
- heavy-duty wire cutters (optional)

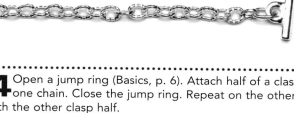

1 earrings • Cut a 1½-in. (3.8cm) piece of memory wire, and make a loop on one end (see step 1 of necklace). String two liquid silver beads, a briolette, and two liquid silver beads. Make a loop on the end of the wire.

2 Cut two 2-in. (5cm) pieces of chain. Attach one piece of chain to each loop of the memory wire. Close the loops.

3 Open a jump ring (Basics). Attach the end of each chain and the loop of an earring wire. Close the jump ring. Make a second earring to match the first.

by **Kim Lucas**

Broaden your appeal

Venetian beads enhance a two-strand necklace and earrings

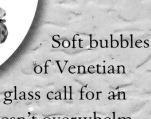

Soft bubbles of Venetian glass call for an airy setting that doesn't overwhelm. Crystals accent the blue and green hues, while gold-lined seed beads mimic the ribbons of sparkle. The focus remains on the front of the necklace as the strands taper on each side. The earring shape balances with the angle of your chin.

SUPPLY LIST

necklace
- **3** Venetian blown-glass beads: 25mm oval bead and **2** 18–21mm round beads
- **2** 8mm round crystals
- **11–13** 6mm bicone crystals
- **10–12** 5mm round glass beads
- **10–14** 6º seed beads
- 5g 11º gold-lined seed beads
- **8** 6mm flat spacers
- flexible beading wire, .014 or .015
- **2** crimp beads
- toggle clasp
- chainnose or crimping pliers
- diagonal wire cutters

earrings
- **2** 22mm round hammered-metal components with three holes at the bottom
- **6** 6mm round crystals in three colors
- **2** 5mm round glass beads
- **6** 5mm faceted rondelles in three colors
- **8** 4mm flat spacers
- **6** 1½-in. (3.8cm) 22-gauge head pins
- pair of earring wires
- chainnose pliers
- roundnose pliers
- diagonal wire cutters

1 **necklace** • Determine the finished length of your necklace. (This one is 17 in./43cm.) Add 6 in. (15cm) and cut two pieces of beading wire to that length. Center a flat spacer, the oval Venetian glass bead, and a spacer on the first wire.

2 On each end of the first wire, string: bicone crystal, six 11º seed beads, 6º seed bead, six 11ºs, 5mm round bead, six 11ºs, spacer.

EDITOR'S TIP
Buy round crystals or Czech glass beads individually rather than by the strand. You'll be able to find great complements to the colors in the Venetian glass.

3 HEART face

3 On the second wire, center a bicone. On each end, string: six 11ºs, 6º, six 11ºs, 5mm round, 12 11ºs. String each end of the wire through the spacers on the first strand.

4 On each end, over both strands, string: bicone, spacer, round Venetian glass bead, spacer, bicone.

5 On one side, separate the strands. On each strand, string six 11ºs. String a 5mm round over both strands. String six 11ºs on each strand, then an 8mm round crystal over both strands. String six 11ºs on each strand, then a bicone over both. Repeat on the other side.

6 On one side, string six 11ºs on each strand, then a 5mm round over both strands. String six 11ºs on each strand, then a 6º over both. String six 11ºs on each strand, then a bicone over both. Repeat on the other side. Repeat the pattern until the necklace is within 1 in. (2.5cm) of the desired length.

7 On one end, over both strands, string a 6º, a crimp bead, a 6º, and half of a clasp. Go back through the beads just strung and tighten the wires. Repeat on the other end. Check the fit, and add or remove beads from each end if necessary. Crimp the crimp beads (Basics, p. 6) and trim the excess wire.

1 **earrings** • On a head pin, string a round crystal, a spacer, and a rondelle. Make a plain loop (Basics) above the top bead. Repeat to make a second dangle. On a third head pin, string: round crystal, spacer, 5mm round bead, spacer, rondelle. Make a plain loop above the top bead.

2 Open the loop (Basics) of the longest dangle. Attach it to the bottom center hole of a metal component. Close the loop. Attach a dangle to each of the two remaining holes of the component.

3 Open the loop of an earring wire. Attach the top hole of the component and close the loop. Make a second earring the mirror image of the first.

Wide, groovy beads make for a flattering retro-chic ensemble

Width style

EDITOR'S TIP
A shorter necklace is another face-flattering option. String an odd number of large square beads at the center of the necklace to ensure that it drapes properly.

by Jane Konkel

Show off your sense of style with mod, 60s-inspired beads. To give the illusion of a more prominent chin, string large square beads along the base of your necklace. Maintain this balance by adding smaller square beads on the sides. Include earrings, with the largest bead at the bottom, for a becoming set.

SUPPLY LIST

necklace
- 16-in. (41cm) strand 35mm flat wood square beads (wood beads from Beads and Pieces, 707-765-2890, beadsandpieces.com)
- 16-in. (41cm) strand 16mm flat wood square beads
- 16-in. (41cm) strand 6mm wood cube beads
- **6–10** 10 x 24mm batik-style horn rondelles (Embroidered Soul, 740-965-4851, embroideredsoul.com)
- **8–12** 9mm wood rondelles
- **48–56** 5mm flat square spacers
- **4** 3mm round spacers
- flexible beading wire, .014 or .015
- **2** crimp beads
- toggle clasp
- chainnose or crimping pliers
- diagonal wire cutters

earrings
- **2** 16mm flat wood square beads
- **2** 9mm wood rondelles
- **2** 6mm wood cube beads
- **4** 5mm flat square spacers
- **2** 3mm round spacers
- 6 in. (15cm) 22-gauge half-hard wire
- **2** 1½-in. (3.8cm) head pins
- pair of lever-back earring wires
- chainnose pliers
- roundnose pliers
- diagonal wire cutters

1 **necklace** • Determine the finished length of your necklace. (This one is 28 in./71cm.) Add 6 in. (15cm) and cut a piece of beading wire to that length. String: two 5mm spacers, 24mm rondelle, two 5mm spacers, 35mm square bead, two 5mm spacers, 24mm rondelle, two 5mm spacers.

2 On each end, string a 35mm square bead, two 5mm spacers, a 24mm rondelle, and two 5mm spacers. Repeat twice.

3 On each end, string: 16mm square bead, 5mm spacer, cube bead, 9mm rondelle, cube, 5mm spacer. Repeat until the necklace is within 1 in. (2.5cm) of the desired length.

4 On each end, string a 3mm spacer, a crimp bead, a 3mm spacer, and half of a clasp. Go back through the beads just strung and tighten the wire. Check the fit, and add or remove beads from each end if necessary. Crimp the crimp beads (Basics, p. 6) and trim the excess wire.

1 **earrings** • String a 16mm square bead and a 3mm spacer on a head pin. Make a plain loop (Basics) above the spacer.

2 Cut a 3-in. (7.6cm) piece of wire. Make a plain loop at one end. Open the loop and attach the bead unit. Close the loop.

3 String a 5mm spacer, a 9mm rondelle, a cube bead, and a 5mm spacer. Make a plain loop above the top bead.

4 Open the loop (Basics) of an earring wire and attach the dangle. Close the loop. Make a second earring to match the first.

Rugged finery

Irregularly cut gemstones
lend a lavish look to an
optimal face shape

by Paulette Biedenbender

The proportional features of an oval face give you fashion carte blanche. Consider a necklace with stones that celebrate this versatility. Juxtapose the rugged cut with the soft sheen of mother-of-pearl and Peruvian opals. It's the perfect fusion of sophistication and natural elements.

1 necklace • Determine the finished length of the short strand of your necklace. (The short strand in this necklace is 17 in./43cm.) Add 6 in. (15cm) and cut a piece of beading wire to that length. Cut another piece 3 in. (7.6cm) longer.
On the long wire, center a nugget. On each end, string a bicone crystal, a cylinder bead, a bicone, and a nugget.

2 On each end of the long wire, string: bicone, three chips, bicone, five cylinders, bicone.

3 On the short wire, string nine chips. Center the beads on the wire.

4 On each end of the short wire, string a bicone, three cylinders, and a bicone.

5 On each end of the short wire, string seven chips and a bicone.

6 On each side, over both wires, string three chips, a bicone, three cylinders, and a bicone. String chips until the strand is within 2 in. (5cm) of the desired length.

7 On each side, over both wires, string a spacer, a crimp bead, a spacer, and half of a clasp. Go back through the beads just strung and tighten the wires. Check the fit, and add or remove beads from each end if necessary. Crimp the crimp beads (Basics, p. 6) and trim the excess wire. If desired, place a crimp cover over the crimp bead, and gently close it with chainnose pliers.

1 earrings • On a head pin, string a bicone crystal, a cylinder bead, and a bicone. Make a plain loop (Basics) above the top bead. Make a total of three bead units.

2 Cut a 6-in. (15cm) piece of wire. Wrap the center of the wire around the largest part of a pair of roundnose pliers. Bring both ends over the top jaw, forming an X above the pliers.

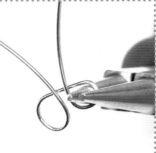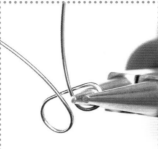

3 On each side of the center loop, approximately ¼ in. (6mm) from the X, make a loop with the middle part of the roundnose pliers.

4 Bring the wires together above the center loop. Wrap one end around the other as if wrapping above a top-drilled bead (Basics).

5 String three bicones on the wire. Make the first half of a wrapped loop (Basics) above the top bead. Attach the loop of an earring post and complete the wraps.

6 Open the loop (Basics) of a bead unit and attach it to the center loop. Close the loop. Attach the remaining bead units to the outer loops. Make a second earring to match the first.

Connect chain and
faceted beads in varying
shades of one color

Take shape

by Kerry Melson

Here's an opportunity to perfect your wrapped loops
while creating a necklace-and-earring set suitable for
an oval face. Instead of purchasing a premade
pendant, why not substitute a fiber-optic bead and
crystals? Finish by attaching dangles to various
links of chain. You will be pleased with
your skills as well as with the results,
so make a quick pair of earrings
to match.

1 **necklace** • Cut a 2½-in. (6.4cm) piece of wire. Make the first half of a wrapped loop (Basics, p. 6) at one end. String: round crystal, flat spacer, 10–12mm bead, spacer, round. Make the first half of a wrapped loop. Make a total of ten to 12 bead units.

2 Cut nine 1-in. (2.5cm) pieces of chain. Attach a loop of a bead unit to a chain. Continue attaching the remaining bead units and chains until you have connected all the bead units. (These necklaces are 16 in./41cm.) End with a bead unit. Check the fit and add or remove chain units or bead units if necessary. Complete the wraps.

3 To make a bead dangle: Cut a 2½-in. (6.4cm) piece of wire. Make a wrapped loop at one end. String: bicone crystal, spacer, fiber-optic bead, spacer, bicone. Make the first half of a wrapped loop above the top bead.

4 String a bicone on a head pin. Make a plain loop (Basics) above the bead. Make a total of three bicone units. Cut a ½-in. (1.3cm) piece of chain. Open the loop of a bead unit and attach it to a chain link. Attach the remaining bead units to the chain. Repeat to make a second chain dangle.

5 Attach each chain dangle to the loop of the bead dangle. Attach the loop to the center link of the necklace. Complete the wraps.

1 earrings • Cut a 2½-in. (6.4cm) piece of wire. Make a wrapped loop (Basics) at one end. String a spacer, a 10–12mm bead, and a spacer. Make the first half of a wrapped loop.

2 Cut a 1-in. (2.5cm) piece of chain. Attach the bead unit's loop to the chain and complete the wraps.

6 String a round crystal on a head pin. Make a plain loop above the crystal. Repeat with the remaining head pins and round crystals.
   Attach three bead units to each chain segment.

3 String a round crystal on a head pin. Make a plain loop (Basics) above the crystal. Repeat to make two more units. Open the loop of each and attach it to a chain link. Close the loop.

4 Open the loop (Basics) of an earring wire and attach the dangle. Close the loop. Make a second earring to match the first.

7 Use a split ring (Basics) to attach half of a clasp and the loop of one end of the necklace. Repeat on the other end.

SUPPLY LIST

necklace
- **10–12** 10–12mm faceted glass beads
- 6-in. (15cm) strand 4mm round Czech fire-polished crystals
- **8** 4mm bicone crystals
- 4–6mm fiber-optic bead
- **22–26** 4–5mm flat spacers
- 28–34 in. (71–86cm) 24-gauge half-hard wire

- 10–14 in. (25–36cm) chain, 4mm links
- **36** 1½-in. (3.8cm) head pins
- **2** 4–6mm split rings
- toggle clasp
- chainnose pliers
- roundnose pliers
- diagonal wire cutters
- split-ring pliers (optional)

earrings
- **2** 10–12mm faceted glass beads

- **6** 4mm round Czech fire-polished crystals
- **4** 4–5mm flat spacers
- 5 in. (13cm) 24-gauge half-hard wire
- 2 in. (5cm) chain, 4mm links
- **6** 1½-in. (3.8cm) head pins
- pair of earring wires
- chainnose pliers
- roundnose pliers
- diagonal wire cutters

EDITOR'S TIP
Any type of 10–12mm bead will work with this necklace. However, faceted beads will add the most dimension to your piece.

Get the best of both worlds

Dress up with sparkling crystals on choker- and opera-length strands

by Lindsay Haedt

This glamorous necklace takes advantage of your ideal face shape by combining the horizontal lines recommended for a heart-shaped face with the length that complements a round or square face. Nobody can pull it off like you can, so flaunt this multiple-length look with confidence and ease. Add long, eye-catching earrings, and this jewelry will shine almost as much as you do.

1 necklace • For the long strand, cut 14 1½-in. (3.8cm) pieces of chain, beginning and ending with a large link. For the short strand, cut six 1½-in. (3.8cm) pieces of chain, beginning and ending with a large link. (The strands in this necklace are 16 in./41cm and 35 in./89cm, with seven and 15 crystal units, respectively.)

2 Cut 12 2-in. (5cm) pieces of wire. Make the first half of a wrapped loop (Basics, p. 6) on one end of a wire. String a bicone crystal and make the first half of a wrapped loop above the bead. Repeat for all wires.

3 Cut 10 2½-in. (6.4cm) pieces of wire. Make the first half of a wrapped loop on one end of a wire. String a bead cap, a round crystal, and a bead cap. Make the first half of a wrapped loop above the bead cap. Repeat for all wires.

4 For each strand, attach a 1½-in. (3.8cm) chain to one loop of a bicone unit and to one loop of a round-crystal unit. Complete the wraps, leaving each end loop unwrapped.

5 Continue attaching crystal units and chains, alternating bicone and round-crystal units. End with a bicone unit, leaving each end loop unwrapped.

6 Check the fit, allowing 2–4 in. (5–10cm) for finishing. Cut four 1–2-in. (2.5–5cm) pieces of chain. On each end, attach a chain to the end loop of a bicone unit. Complete the wraps.

For each strand, open a jump ring (Basics) and attach the chain to half of a clasp. Close the jump ring.

SUPPLY LIST

necklace
- **10** 10mm round crystals
- **12** 6mm bicone crystals
- **20** 8mm bead caps
- 49 in. (1.2m) 22-gauge half-hard wire
- 40–44 in. (1–1.1m) large-and-small-link chain, 3–4mm links
- **4** 4mm jump rings
- box clasp
- chainnose pliers
- roundnose pliers
- diagonal wire cutters

earrings
- **2** 10mm round crystals
- **6** 6mm bicone crystals
- **4** 8mm bead caps
- 2½ in. (6.4cm) large-and-small-link chain, 3–4mm links
- **8** 1½-in. (3.8cm) head pins
- pair of earring wires
- chainnose pliers
- roundnose pliers
- diagonal wire cutters

EDITOR'S TIP

For a balanced necklace, make sure each strand has a centered round-crystal unit.

1 earrings • Cut a 1¼-in. (3.2cm) piece of chain. Begin and end with a large link. Open the loop (Basics) of an earring wire. Attach the chain and close the loop.

2 String a bicone crystal on a head pin. Make the first half of a wrapped loop (Basics) above the bead. Make a total of three bicone units.

3 Attach a bicone unit to the top chain link. Complete the wraps. Repeat twice, alternating sides and attaching bicone units to the next two large links.

4 String a bead cap, a round crystal, and a bead cap on a head pin. Make the first half of a wrapped loop and attach it to the last chain link. Complete the wraps. Make a second earring to match the first.

Leafy latitude

An oval face gives you the freedom to experiment with unusual beads • by Cathy Jakicic

Beads in wine-country colors combine with lush resin leaves for an intoxicating necklace of any length. The twisting second strand mimics a vine, and simple dangle earrings are well-balanced top notes.

1 **necklace** • String a 3mm bicone crystal, a small leaf, and a medium leaf on a head pin. Bend the head pin at a right angle and string two 8º seed beads.

Make a wrapped loop (Basics, p. 6) perpendicular to the leaves. Make a total of four dangles.

EDITOR'S TIP Use copper-colored findings to complement deep purples and greens.

2 Determine the finished length of your necklace. (This one is 16 in./41cm.) Add 6 in. (15cm) and cut a piece of beading wire to that length. Center the large leaf on the wire.

On each end, string six 8ºs, an 11º, an 8º, and an 11º. Repeat the pattern.

3 On each end, string three 8ºs, a leaf dangle, three 8ºs, an 11º, an 8º, and an 11º.

4 **a** On each end, string six 8ºs, an 11º, an 8º, and an 11º.

b Repeat step 3, then repeat step 4a until the strand is within ½ in. (1.3cm) of the desired length. Tape the ends.

5 Cut a piece of beading wire 6 in. (15cm) longer than the first. Make a leaf dangle as in step 1, omitting the medium leaf and using a 4mm bicone crystal. Center 17 11ºs, the small leaf dangle, and 17 11ºs on the wire.

6 Center the small leaf dangle on the first strand. String one end of the second strand through the first 8º that is between two 11ºs on the first strand, as shown. Repeat on the other side.

7 On each end of the second strand, string five 11ºs, a pearl, and 13 11ºs. String the wire through the second 8º between two 11ºs on the first strand. Repeat.

8 On each end of the second strand, string 19 11ºs. String the wire through the second 8º between two 11ºs on the first strand.

SUPPLY LIST

necklace
- 28 x 39mm resin leaf bead, top drilled (all resin beads from Dee's Place, 952-492-2493, beadsbydee.com)
- **4** 25 x 27mm resin leaf beads
- **5** 15 x 15mm resin grape-leaf beads
- **4** 6mm pearls
- 4mm bicone crystal
- **4** 3mm bicone crystals
- 4g 8º seed beads
- 5g 11º seed beads
- flexible beading wire, .014 or .015
- **5** 2-in. (5cm) copper head pins
- **2** crimp beads
- clasp
- chainnose pliers
- roundnose pliers
- diagonal wire cutters
- crimping pliers (optional)

earrings
- **4** 15 x 15mm resin grape-leaf beads
- **4** 4mm bicone crystals
- **4** 2-in. (5cm) copper head pins
- pair of earring wires
- chainnose pliers
- roundnose pliers
- diagonal wire cutters

9 **a** On each end of the second strand, string 11ºs until the strand is a total of ½ in. (1.3cm) longer than the first strand (¼ in./6mm on each end).

b Remove the tape from the first strand. On each end, over both strands, string a crimp bead and half of a clasp. Go back through the beads just strung and tighten the wires. Check the fit, and add or remove beads from each end if necessary. Crimp the crimp beads (Basics) and trim the excess wire.

1 **earrings** • String a bicone crystal and a small leaf on a head pin. Bend the head pin at a right angle, and make a wrapped loop (Basics) approximately 1 in. (2.5cm) above the leaf. Make a second dangle with a wrapped loop ¾ in. (1.9cm) above the leaf.

2 Open an earring wire and attach the dangles. Close the wire. Make a second earring to match the first.

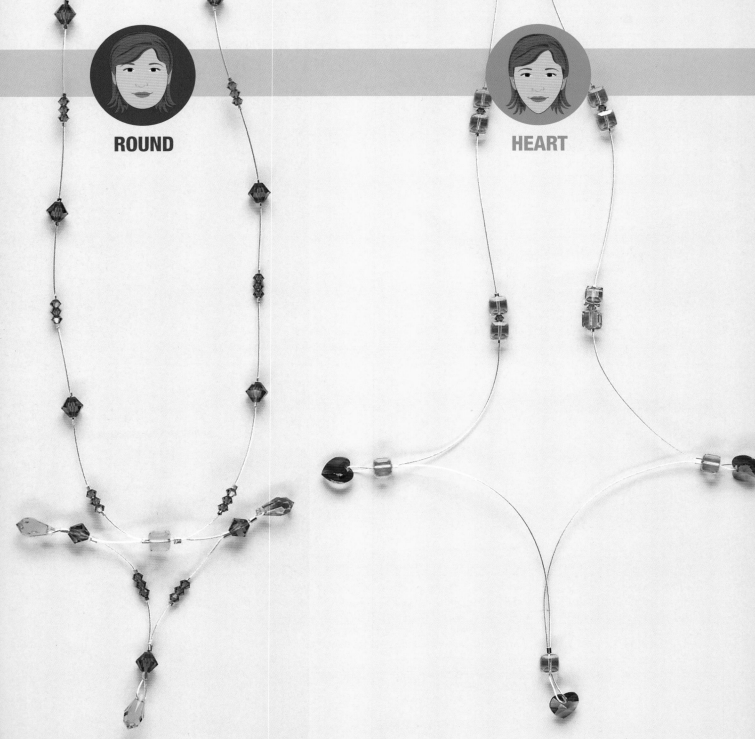

Versatile

ROUND

HEART

crystals

Crystal creations on
sterling silver beading
wire flatter any face shape

SQUARE

OVAL

by Cathy Jakicic

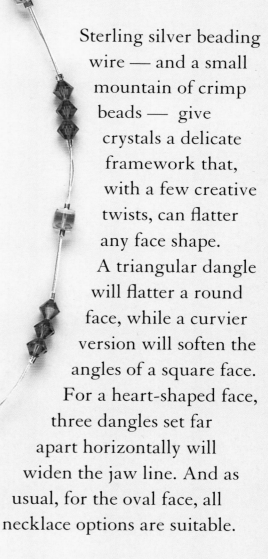

Sterling silver beading
wire — and a small
mountain of crimp
beads — give
crystals a delicate
framework that,
with a few creative
twists, can flatter
any face shape.

A triangular dangle
will flatter a round
face, while a curvier
version will soften the
angles of a square face.
For a heart-shaped face,
three dangles set far
apart horizontally will
widen the jaw line. And as
usual, for the oval face, all
necklace options are suitable.

1 round face necklace • Determine the finished length of your necklace. (This one is 36 in./ 0.9m.) Add 10 in. (25cm) and cut a piece of beading wire to that length. Center a drop crystal on the wire. Over both wires, string a crimp bead, a 6mm bicone crystal, and a crimp bead. Crimp the crimp beads (Basics, p. 6).

2 On each end, ½ in. (1.3cm) from the last crimp bead strung, string a microcrimp bead, three 3mm bicone crystals, and a microcrimp bead. Crimp the microcrimp beads.

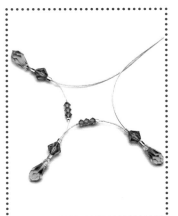

3 On each end, ½ in. (1.3cm) from the last crimp bead strung, string a crimp bead, a 6mm bicone, a crimp bead, and a drop. Go back through the crimp beads and the 6mm bicone. Crimp the crimp beads.

4 On one end, string a crimp bead, a cube crystal, and a crimp bead. String the other end through the beads from the opposite direction. Tighten the wires until they form a triangle. Crimp the crimp beads.

5 a On each end, ½ in. (1.3cm) from the last crimp bead strung, string a microcrimp, three 3mm bicones, and a microcrimp bead. Crimp the microcrimp beads.
  b On each end, 1 in. (2.5cm) from the last microcrimp bead strung, string a microcrimp bead, a 6mm bicone, and a microcrimp bead. Crimp the microcrimp beads.
  c Repeat steps 5a and 5b until the necklace is within 2 in. (5cm) of the desired length.

6 On one end, string: microcrimp bead, 6mm bicone, crimp bead, 6mm bicone, lobster claw clasp. Go back through the last beads strung and tighten the wire. Repeat on the other end, substituting a soldered jump ring for the clasp. Crimp the crimp beads and trim the excess wire.

1 a heart-shaped face necklace • Determine the finished length of your necklace. (This one is 25 in./64cm.) Add 8 in. (20cm) and cut a piece of beading wire to that length. Center a heart-shaped crystal on the wire. Over both ends, string a cube crystal and a crimp bead. Crimp the crimp bead (Basics).
  b On each end, 5 in. (13cm) from the crimp bead last strung, string a crimp bead, a cube, and a heart. Go back through the cube and the crimp bead. Crimp the crimp bead (Basics).

2 On each end, 2¼ in. (5.7cm) from the last crimp bead strung, string a microcrimp bead, a cube, a 3mm bicone crystal, a cube, and a microcrimp bead. Crimp the microcrimp beads. Repeat until the necklace is within 2 in. (5cm) of the desired length.
  Finish the necklace as in step 6 of the round-face necklace, substituting cubes for the bicones.

1 **square face necklace** • Determine the finished length of your necklace. (This one is 33 in./84cm.) Add 10 in. (25cm) and cut a piece of beading wire to that length. On the wire, center: microcrimp bead, bicone crystal, cube crystal, bicone, microcrimp bead. Crimp the microcrimp beads (Basics).

2 On one end, string: crimp bead, bicone, cube, bicone, crimp. String the other end through the beads from the opposite direction. Tighten the wires until they form a circle approximately 2 in. (5cm) in diameter. Crimp the crimp beads.

3 On each end, 2¼ in. (5.7cm) from the last crimp bead strung, string a microcrimp bead, a cube, a bicone, a cube, and a microcrimp bead. Crimp the microcrimp beads. Repeat until the necklace is within 4 in. (10cm) of the desired length.

Finish the necklace as in step 6 of the round-face necklace, substituting cubes for bicones.

1 **oval face necklace** • Determine the finished length of your necklace. (This one is 19 in./48cm.) Add 6 in. (15cm) and cut two pieces of beading wire to that length. On one wire, center a heart-shaped crystal. Over both ends, string a bicone crystal and a crimp bead. Crimp the crimp bead (Basics).

2 **a** String a cube crystal on each end of the wire.
b String the second wire through the two cubes just strung. On each end, string a crimp bead over both wires. Crimp the crimp beads.

3 **a** On each end, 1 in. (2.5cm) from the last crimp bead strung, string a crimp bead, three bicones, and a crimp bead. Crimp the crimp beads.
b On each end, 1 in. (2.5cm) from the last crimp bead strung, string a crimp bead, a cube, and a crimp bead. Crimp the crimp beads.
c Repeat steps 3a and 3b until the necklace is within 8 in. (20cm) of the desired length.

4 Finish the necklace as in step 6 of the round-face necklace, substituting a crimp bead, two 6mm spacers and a crimp bead for the 6mm bicone pattern.

EDITOR'S TIP
Check the necklace's fit at each step. Once the beads are crimped, it is difficult to remove them.

SUPPLY LIST

all necklaces
• sterling silver flexible beading wire, .019
• chainnose pliers
• diagonal wire cutters
• microcrimping and crimping pliers (optional)

round face necklace
• 3 6 x 2mm drop crystals
• **19–23** 6mm bicone crystals
• **48–60** 3mm bicone crystals
• 6mm cube crystal
• **60–80** microcrimp beads
• **10** crimp beads
• lobster claw clasp and soldered jump ring

heart-shaped face necklace
• 3 10mm heart-shaped crystals
• **15–19** 6mm cube crystals
• **4–6** 3mm bicone crystals
• **10–14** microcrimp beads
• **5** crimp beads
• lobster claw clasp and soldered jump ring

square face necklace
• **22–26** 6mm cube crystals
• **12–14** 6mm bicone crystals
• **18-22** microcrimp beads
• **6** crimp beads
• lobster claw clasp and soldered jump ring

oval face necklace
• 10mm heart-shaped crystal
• **13–19** 6mm bicone crystals
• **6–8** 6mm cube crystals
• **4** 6mm silver spacers
• **23–27** crimp beads
• lobster claw clasp and soldered jump ring

Necklines

5
Round
PAGE 52

With a round neckline, it's best to keep the lines of your jewelry simple. A short necklace that echoes the line of the garment works well. Similarly, the earrings should not overpower the necklace. Stay away from dramatic dangles in both the necklace and the earrings.

6
V-neck
PAGE 61

A V-neck offers the opportunity to show off beautiful pendants and dramatic dangles. Keep the focus in the front to avoid stringing a necklace that fights with the centered symmetry of the V. Dangling earrings will further accentuate long lines.

7
Turtleneck
PAGE 71

There are two main things to remember with a turtleneck: the necklace should be long enough that it doesn't crowd the collar, and should use beads that are bold enough in color, size, or shape (or all three) that they stand out on fabric. Keep earrings short so they don't touch the high collar.

8
Strapless
PAGE 81

Like the classic oval face, a strapless neckline offers a wealth of options. Take advantage of the wide-open canvas to showcase a striking choker, bold pendant, or delicate strand. Earrings of any length work as long as they are kept in proportion with the necklace.

All necklines
PAGE 90

For a necklace that fits well with any neckline, see "Wardrobe wonder."

Center of attention

Keep all eyes on you with a Victorian choker that focuses on a stunning clasp

by Cathy Jakicic

Four strands of freshwater pearls in different shades and shapes create an elegant backdrop for a clasp too beautiful to stay backstage. Be sure to string pearl strands with only subtle differences so your well-chosen clasp gets the undivided attention it deserves. The necklace's choker length, accented by short earring dangles, won't compete with a round neckline.

1 **necklace** • Determine the finished length of your necklace. (This one is 14 in./36cm.) Add 6 in. (15cm) and cut four pieces of beading wire to that length. On each wire, string pearls until each strand is within 1 in. (2.5cm) of the desired length. Tape the ends.

EDITOR'S TIP

Pearls have tiny holes. You'll need very fine beading wire to go through them twice when finishing the necklace. If you don't want to use thinner wire, finish with large-hole spacers on both ends of your strands.

2 **a** Remove the tape from one end of one strand. String a microcrimp bead and the top loop of a clasp. Go back through the beads just strung and tighten the wire. Repeat with the remaining strands, attaching two strands to each loop of half of the clasp.

b Repeat step 2a on the other side. Check the fit and add or remove pearls if necessary. Crimp the crimp beads (Basics, p. 6) and trim the excess wire.

SUPPLY LIST

necklace
- focal two-strand box clasp (Sojourner, 609-397-8849, sojourner.biz)
- **4** 16-in. (41cm) strands 8–10mm pearls, assorted shapes and colors
- flexible beading wire, .010 or .012
- **8** microcrimp beads
- chainnose or micro-crimping pliers
- diagonal wire cutters

earrings
- **8** 8–10mm pearls, **2** from each strand used in the necklace
- **8** 1½-in. (3.8cm) decorative head pins
- pair of earring wires
- chainnose pliers
- roundnose pliers
- diagonal wire cutters

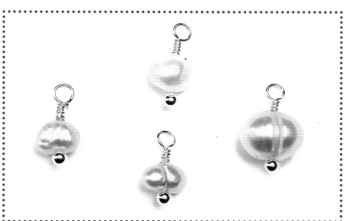

1 **earrings** • String a pearl from each strand on a decorative head pin. Make a wrapped loop (Basics) above each pearl.

2 Open the loop (Basics) of an earring wire and attach the dangles. Close the loop. Make a second earring to match the first.

A cut above

Combine muted, angular gemstones with bright satin beads for an easy necklace and earrings

by Jane Konkel

Before stringing this necklace, take stock of the necklines in your wardrobe. Do your round necklines tend to sit at your collarbone, or do they plunge? When determining the length of your necklace, keep in mind that this piece is most flattering when it falls just above the collar of your round neckline.

1 **necklace** • Determine the finished length of your necklace. (This necklace is 17 in./43cm.) Add 6 in. (15cm) and cut a piece of beading wire to that length. String a nugget and a spacer, repeating as desired. End with a nugget. Center the beads.

2 On one end, string: spacer, satin bead, spacer, satin bead, spacer.

3 On the other end, string a spacer, a satin bead, and a spacer.
String a nugget and a spacer, repeating for approximately 4 in. (10cm). End with a nugget.

4 On the other end, string approximately 4½ in. (11.4cm) of rondelles.

5 On each end, string a spacer, a crimp bead, a spacer, and half of a clasp. Go back through the beads just strung and tighten the wire. Check the fit, and add or remove beads from each end if necessary. Crimp the crimp beads (Basics, p. 6) and trim the excess wire.

SUPPLY LIST

necklace
- **3** 16mm satin beads (Rupa B. Designs, rupab.com)
- **16-in.** (41cm) strand 14 x 20mm faceted gemstone nuggets
- **16-in.** (41cm) strand 4mm faceted rondelles
- **15–20** 5mm spacers
- flexible beading wire, .014 or .015
- **2** crimp beads
- toggle clasp
- chainnose or crimping pliers
- diagonal wire cutters

earrings
- **2** 16mm satin beads (Rupa B. Designs)
- **2** 5mm spacers
- **2** 2-in. (5cm) decorative head pins
- pair of decorative earring wires
- chainnose pliers
- roundnose pliers
- diagonal wire cutters

1 **earrings** • String a satin bead and a spacer on a decorative head pin. Make a wrapped loop (Basics) above the top bead.

2 Open an earring wire and attach the dangle. Close the wire. Make a second earring to match the first.

by Paulette Biedenbender

Buttoned-up choker

Crystals and rhinestones accent a two-strand pearl necklace

Good things come in small packages. Proof is in this necklace of precious button pearls. Crystals add brilliance while rhinestone bridges keep the strands in place, giving the necklace a rounded shape. Play up the petite pearls with small-scale earrings. Make short, dangly earrings like the ones shown here, or opt for a single pearl drop on a post.

SUPPLY LIST

necklace

- **2** 16-in. (41cm) strands 3–3.5mm button pearls
- **40–44** 4mm bicone crystals
- **4** 3 x 13mm two-strand rhinestone bridge components
- **8** 3mm round spacers
- flexible beading wire, .014 or .015
- **4** crimp beads
- two-strand clasp
- chainnose or crimping pliers
- diagonal wire cutters

earrings

- **2** 6mm crystal rondelles
- **2** 4mm bicone crystals
- **2** 3–3.5mm button pearls
- **2** 3mm round pearls
- **2** 1½-in. (3.8cm) head pins
- pair of earring posts with ear nuts
- chainnose pliers
- roundnose pliers
- diagonal wire cutters

1a necklace • Determine the finished length of your necklace. (This one is 16½ in./41.9cm.) Add 6 in. (15cm) and cut a piece of beading wire to that length. Cut a second piece 1 in. (2.5cm) longer than the first.

b On the shorter wire (inner strand), string ¾ in. (1.9cm) of pearls. Center the pearls on the wire. On each end, string a bicone crystal, ¾ in. (1.9cm) of pearls, and a bicone.

c On the longer wire (outer strand), center a bicone. On each end, string ¾ in. (1.9cm) of pearls, a bicone, four pearls, and a bicone.

2 On each side, string the corresponding hole of a rhinestone bridge component.

3a On each end of the inner strand, string: bicone, ¾ in. (1.9cm) of pearls, bicone, ¾ in. (1.9cm) of pearls, bicone.

b On each end of the outer strand, string: bicone, four pearls, bicone, 1 in. (2.5cm) of pearls, bicone, four pearls, bicone. On each side, string the corresponding hole of a rhinestone bridge.

4a On each end of the inner strand, string a bicone and ¾ in. (1.9cm) of pearls. Repeat until the strand is within 1 in. (2.5cm) of the desired length.

b On each end of the outer strand, string a bicone and four pearls. String a bicone and ¾ in. (1.9cm) of pearls, repeating until the strand is within 1 in. (2.5cm) of the desired length.

5 On each end, string a round spacer, a crimp bead, a spacer, and the corresponding loop of half of a clasp. Go back through the beads just strung and tighten the wires. Check the fit and add or remove beads if necessary. Crimp the crimp beads (Basics, p. 6) and trim the excess wire.

1 earrings • On a head pin, string a round pearl, a button pearl, a rondelle, and a bicone crystal. Make the first half of a wrapped loop (Basics) above the crystal.

2 Attach the dangle's loop to the loop of an earring post. Complete the wraps. Make a second earring to match the first.

EDITOR'S TIP

Before crimping, check the fit of the necklace while it's in a circular position (as it would be worn). This will ensure flexibility and a graceful drape.

by Sara Strauss

Circle of light

Teardrops and faceted
rondelles sparkle in
a choker-length necklace
and chain earrings

For work or for play, pair a candy-colored briolette necklace
and earrings with a jewel-neck top. The necklace's rounded shape will
match effortlessly with the neckline of a favorite tee or sweater.
Keep the necklace short and sweet by dotting just a few beads along
lengths of chain. Add earrings with a trio of beaded drops to
make your style statement with just a few elements.

1 **necklace** • Cut a 3-in. (7.6cm) piece of wire. Make the first half of a wrapped loop (Basics, p. 6) at one end. String a briolette and make the first half of a wrapped loop at the other end. Make a total of five briolette units.

2 Cut a 3-in. (7.6cm) piece of wire. Make the first half of a wrapped loop at one end. String two rondelles in different colors, and make the first half of a wrapped loop at the other end. Make a total of six rondelle units.

3 Cut 12 1-in. (2.5cm) pieces of chain. Attach a piece of chain to each loop of a briolette unit. Complete the wraps.

4 Attach one loop of a rondelle unit to each chain. Complete the wraps of the loops attached to the chains.

5 Continue attaching chains and bead units to each end, alternating briolette and rondelle units, until the necklace is within 1 in. (2.5cm) of the desired length. (This necklace is 16 in./ 41cm.) End with a chain on each side.

6 Check the fit. Add a bead unit or trim links on each end if necessary. Open a 4mm jump ring (Basics) and attach a lobster claw clasp to one chain. Repeat on the other end, substituting a soldered jump ring for the clasp.

EDITOR'S TIP
To make quick work of cutting chain with long links, count the number of links rather than using a ruler to measure each piece.

1 **earrings** • Cut a 3-in. (7.6cm) piece of wire. String a briolette and make a set of wraps above it (Basics). Make the first half of a wrapped loop (Basics) above the wraps.

2 To make a rondelle unit: String a rondelle on a decorative head pin. Make a plain loop (Basics) above the bead. Repeat with a rondelle in a second color.

SUPPLY LIST

necklace

- **5–7** 8 x 12mm briolettes
- **12–16** 5mm faceted rondelles, in two colors
- **3–4** ft. (.9–1.2m) 24-gauge half-hard wire
- **14–18** in. (36–46cm) chain, 3–5mm links
- **2** 4mm jump rings
- lobster claw clasp and soldered jump ring
- chainnose pliers
- roundnose pliers
- diagonal wire cutters

earrings

- **2** 8 x 12mm briolettes
- **4** 5mm faceted rondelles, in two colors
- **2** three-to-one connector bars
- **6** in. (15cm) 24-gauge half-hard wire
- **9–11** in. (23–28cm) chain, 3–5mm links
- **4** 1-in. (2.5cm) decorative head pins
- **6** 3mm jump rings
- pair of earring wires
- chainnose pliers
- roundnose pliers
- diagonal wire cutters

3 Cut three pieces of chain: one long and two short. (These are 1¾ in./ 4.4cm and 1¼ in./3.2cm.)
Attach the briolette unit to the long chain. Complete the wraps. Open the loop of a rondelle unit and attach a short chain. Close the loop. Repeat with the remaining rondelle unit.

4 Open a jump ring (Basics). Attach the briolette dangle's chain to the center loop of a connector bar. Close the jump ring. Use jump rings to attach the rondelle dangles to the outer loops of the connector bar.

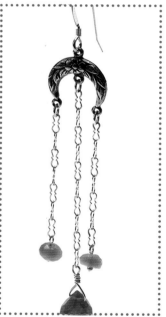

5 Open the loop (Basics) of an earring wire. Attach the top loop of the connector bar and close the loop. Make a second earring the mirror image of the first.

String light and dark shades of assorted beads for a monochromatic necklace and earrings. The delicate necklace chain is choker length, while the elongated dangle cascades into the V of your neckline. See how dramatically you can perk up a simple T-shirt.

Take the plunge

by Denaé Oglesby

Cluster a soft palette of distinctive beads in a Y-necklace and earrings

EDITOR'S TIP
Adjust the length of the chain for the dangle as necessary to avoid losing your necklace in your cleavage — 3 in. (7.6cm) or shorter is usually best.

1 necklace • To make a teardrop or briolette unit: Cut a 2½-in. (6.4cm) piece of wire. String a teardrop and make a set of wraps above the bead (Basics, p. 6). Make the first half of a wrapped loop (Basics) above the wraps. Make a total of four teardrop units.

2 Determine the finished length of your necklace. (These are 18 in./46cm with 3-in./7.6cm dangles.) Cut two pieces of chain: one, necklace length; the other, dangle length. Attach a teardrop unit to the dangle chain's bottom link and to every other link. Complete the wraps.

3 String five gemstone chips on a head pin. Make the first half of a wrapped loop above the top chip. Make two more chip units: one with four chips and one with three.

4 String a crystal or pearl on a head pin. Make the first half of a wrapped loop above the bead. Make a total of 12 units. Attach the chip (from step 3), crystal, and pearl units to the chain, clustering most units near the bottom. Complete the wraps.

5 Cut a 2½-in. (6.4cm) piece of wire. Make the first half of a wrapped loop on one end. String a rondelle, a pearl, and a rondelle. Make the first half of a wrapped loop above the top bead. Attach one loop to the dangle chain and the other loop to the necklace chain's center link. Complete the wraps.

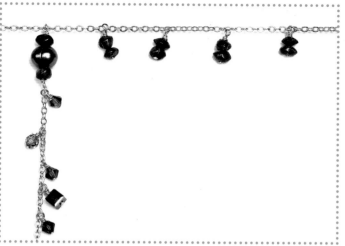

SUPPLY LIST

necklace
- **4** 5 x 12mm teardrops or briolettes
- **4** 6–9mm potato-shaped pearls
- **2** 6mm bicone crystals
- **8–10** 4–6mm crystals, assorted shapes and colors
- **12** 4mm gemstone chips
- **18** 4mm rondelles
- **17½** in. (44.5cm) 24-gauge half-hard wire
- **15–21** in. (38–53cm) chain, 3–4mm links
- **20–26** 1½-in. (3.8cm) 26-gauge head pins
- lobster claw clasp and soldered jump ring
- chainnose pliers
- roundnose pliers
- diagonal wire cutters

earrings
- **2** 5 x 12mm teardrops or briolettes
- **14** 4mm crystals, assorted shapes and colors
- **8** 4mm gemstone chips
- 5 in. (13cm) 24-gauge half-hard wire
- 4 in. (10cm) chain, 3–4mm links
- **18** 1½-in. (3.8cm) 26-gauge head pins
- pair of earring wires
- chainnose pliers
- roundnose pliers
- diagonal wire cutters

6 String two rondelles on a head pin. Make the first half of a wrapped loop above the top rondelle. Make a total of eight rondelle units. Approximately ½ in. (1.3cm) from the necklace's center, attach a rondelle unit to a link. Complete the wraps. Attach the remaining units at ½-in. (1.3cm) intervals, four on each side of the dangle.

7 Check the fit, and trim chain from each end if necessary. Cut a 2½-in. (6.4cm) piece of wire. Make the first half of a wrapped loop on one end. Attach it to one end of the chain and complete the wraps. Repeat on the other end.

8 String a 6mm bicone crystal and make the first half of a wrapped loop next to the crystal. Attach a lobster claw clasp. Complete the wraps. Repeat on the other end, substituting a soldered jump ring for the clasp.

1 **earrings** • Make a teardrop or briolette unit as in step 1 of the necklace. Cut a 2-in. (5cm) piece of chain. Attach the teardrop unit. Complete the wraps.

2 String two gemstone chips on a head pin. Make the first half of a wrapped loop above the top chip. Make a total of two chip units. Attach each to the teardrop unit's loop. Complete the wraps.

3 String a crystal on a head pin. Make the first half of a wrapped loop above the crystal. Make a total of seven crystal units. Attach one to the teardrop unit's loop and two to the chain's bottom link. Attach each remaining unit to the chain, clustering most units near the bottom. Complete the wraps.

4 Open the loop (Basics) of an earring wire and attach the dangle. Close the loop. Make a second earring to match the first.

Drop everything

Cylinder beads replace knots in a toggle-front necklace

by Rupa Balachandar

Buck tradition with a pearl necklace that blends class and sass. Traditionally, pearl strands are knotted. Here, tiny cylinder beads separate the pearls, which attach to a pretty toggle clasp intended for front focus. A dangle suspended from the clasp provides an unexpected twist. Simple drop earrings complement without competing.

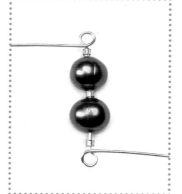

1 **necklace** • Cut a 4-in. (10cm) piece of 22-gauge wire. String the drop bead and make a set of wraps above it as in a top-drilled bead (Basics, p. 6). Make the first half of a wrapped loop (Basics) above the wraps.

2 Cut a 4-in. (10cm) piece of wire. Make the first half of a wrapped loop on one end. String: 11º cylinder bead, pearl, 11º, pearl, 11º. Make the first half of a wrapped loop above the top bead.

3 Attach one loop of the pearl unit to the drop's loop and complete the wraps. Attach the remaining loop to the loop of the ring half of a clasp. Complete the wraps.

4 Determine the necklace's length. (This one is 16 in./ 41cm with a 2½-in./6.4cm dangle.) Add 6 in. (15cm) and cut a piece of beading wire to that length.

String a crimp bead, two 2mm round spacers, and the ring half of a toggle clasp. Go back through the beads just strung and crimp the crimp bead (Basics).

5 String an alternating pattern of pearls and 11ºs, beginning with a pearl, until the necklace is within ½ in. (1.3cm) of the desired length. Check the fit, and add or remove beads if necessary. Finish the necklace as in step 4 using the bar half of the clasp.

1 **earrings** • String a pearl on a head pin and make a plain loop (Basics) above the pearl.

2 Open the loop (Basics), attach one loop of a connector bar, and close the loop. Open the loop of an earring wire, attach the dangle, and close the loop. Make a second earring the mirror image of the first.

SUPPLY LIST

necklace
- 20 x 30mm glass drop bead, top drilled
- 16-in. (41cm) strand 6–9mm potato-shaped pearls
- 1g 11º Japanese cylinder beads
- **4** 2mm round spacers

- flexible beading wire, .014 or .015
- 8 in. (20cm) 22-gauge half-hard wire
- **2** crimp beads
- toggle clasp
- chainnose pliers
- roundnose pliers
- diagonal wire cutters
- crimping pliers (optional)

earrings
- 2 6–9mm potato-shaped pearls
- 2 6 x 20mm connector bars
- 2 1½-in. (3.8cm) head pins
- pair of earring wires
- chainnose pliers
- roundnose pliers
- diagonal wire cutters

EDITOR'S TIP

If you don't have connector bars, make earrings by stringing pearls and cylinder beads on a head pin. Drop earrings accent the vertical line created by the necklace.

Softly framed

Muted pearls and gemstones support an art-glass bead in a triple-strand necklace

by Paulette Biedenbender

Subtle colors of pearls and gemstones reflect the pastel shadings of an art-glass bead. Simply braid the pearl strands around the gemstones to create a setting for the prettiest of beads. The earrings are understated yet stylish, providing just a hint of color on a glimmering earring thread.

SUPPLY LIST

necklace
- art-glass bead (Peggy Prielozny, Bead Needs, 414-529-5211)
- 16-in. (41cm) strand 12mm barrel-shaped gemstones
- 16-in. (41cm) strand 6mm teardrop pearls, top drilled
- 16-in. (41cm) strand 5mm button pearls, top drilled
- 16-in. (41cm) strand 4mm rondelles
- 6mm bicone crystal
- 2 4mm bicone crystals
- 4mm rhinestone ball with loop
- 2g 11º seed beads, in two colors
- 4 3mm round spacers
- flexible beading wire, .014 or .015
- Fireline fishing line, 6 or 8 lb. test
- 2 crimp beads
- 4 bead tips
- three-strand clasp
- beading needle, #12
- chainnose pliers
- diagonal wire cutters
- G-S Hypo Cement
- crimping pliers (optional)

earrings
- 2 6mm round crystals
- 2 4mm bicone crystals
- 2 4mm rondelles
- 6 1-in. (2.5cm) head pins
- pair of earring threads
- chainnose pliers
- roundnose pliers
- diagonal wire cutters

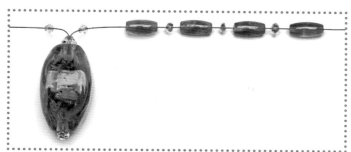

1 **necklace** • Determine the finished length of your necklace. (The long strand in this necklace is 18 in./46cm.) Add 8 in. (20cm) and cut a piece of beading wire to that length. Center a rhinestone ball on the wire.

Over both ends, string the art-glass bead and a 6mm crystal. Separate the wires and string a 4mm crystal on each end.

2 On each end, string a barrel-shaped bead and a rondelle. Repeat until the strand is within 1 in. (2.5cm) of the desired length. End with a rondelle. Tape the ends.

3 Add 6 in. (15cm) to the desired length of the necklace. Double that measurement and cut two pieces of Fireline to that length.

Thread one piece on a needle. Beginning and ending with an 11º seed bead, string an alternating pattern of teardrop pearls and 11ºs until the strand is double the desired length. Repeat on the remaining strand with button pearls and 11ºs in a second color.

> **EDITOR'S TIP**
> Size 1 silk or nylon bead cord can be substituted for the Fireline.

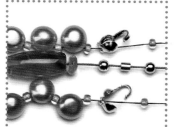

4 Fold each strand of pearls in half so that the folds link, as shown.

5 Position the pearl strands so the gemstone strand hangs approximately 1½ in. (3.8cm) below the fold. On each side, crisscross the pearl strands over and under the gemstone strand until the necklace is within 1 in. (2.5cm) of the desired length.

1 **earrings** • On a head pin, string a rondelle. Make a plain loop (Basics) above the bead. Repeat with a round crystal and a bicone crystal.

6 On each end of each pearl strand, string a bead tip and an 11º. On the ends of the gemstone strand, string a spacer, a crimp bead, and a spacer. Check the fit, allowing 1 in. (2.5cm) for the clasp, and add or remove beads from each end if necessary.

On each end of each pearl strand, tie a knot around the 11º. Glue the knot and trim the Fireline to ⅛ in. (3mm). Using chainnose pliers, close the bead tip around the knot.

7 On each end of each pearl strand, attach a bead tip's loop to an outer loop of half of a clasp. Close the bead tip's loop. Remove the tape. String the gemstone strand's wire through the remaining clasp loop and go back through the last beads strung. Crimp the crimp beads (Basics, p. 6) and trim the excess wire. Repeat on the other end.

2 Open the loop (Basics) of an earring thread. Attach the three dangles and close the loop. Make a second earring to match the first.

Get to the point

A clever multistrand variation creates an original necklace and matching earrings

by Juli Martin

Make a statement about fashion and creativity with this delicate mix of seed beads, crystals, and pearls. Well-placed spacer bars and crimp beads make the outer strands converge, leading the eye to the briolette dangles. So, the next time you are dressing for a big night, make a point of being stunning. This necklace's width diminishes near the nape, but its impact never will.

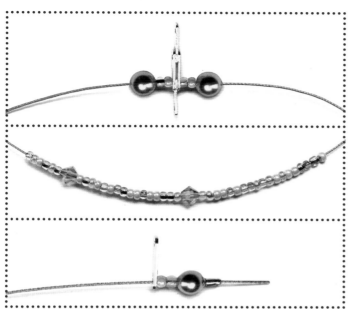

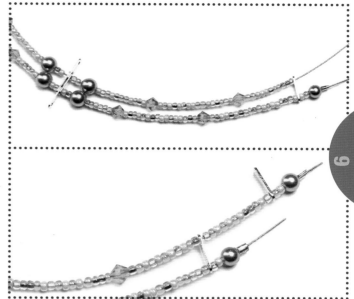

1a **necklace • bottom strand:** Cut a 10-in. (25cm) piece of beading wire. String the third hole of the four-hole spacer bar and center it. On each end, string two 11º seed beads and a 5mm pearl.

b On each end, string: 6 11ºs, 4mm bicone crystal, 16 11ºs, 4mm bicone, 19 11ºs.

c On each end, string a two-hole spacer bar, two 11ºs, a 4mm pearl, and a crimp bead.
Crimp the crimp bead (Basics, p. 6). Trim the excess wire.

2a **middle strand:** Cut an 11-in. (28cm) piece of beading wire. String the second hole of the four-hole spacer bar and center it.

On each end, string: 2 11ºs, 5mm pearl, 11 11ºs, 4mm bicone, 16 11ºs, 4mm bicone, 11 11ºs, second hole of the two-hole spacer bar from step 1c.

b On each end, string: 12 11ºs, two-hole spacer bar, 2 11ºs, 4mm pearl, crimp bead. Crimp as in step 1c.

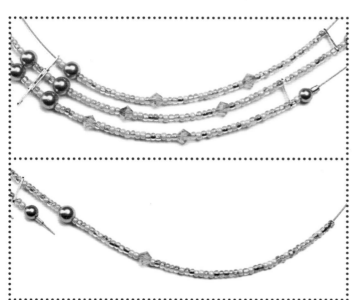

3a **top strand:** Determine the length of the top strand of your necklace. (This one is 13 in./33cm.) Add 6 in. (15cm) and cut a piece of beading wire to that length. String the first hole of the four-hole spacer bar and center it.

On each end, string: two 11ºs, 5mm pearl, 15 11ºs, 4mm bicone, 16 11ºs, 4mm bicone, 16 11ºs, second hole of the two-hole spacer bar from step 2b.

b On each end, string: 10 11ºs, 5mm pearl, 16 11ºs, 4mm bicone. String 11ºs until the strand is within ½ in. (1.3cm) of the desired length.

EDITOR'S TIP
If finding the right size four-hole spacer bar in gold proves difficult, try making one using four 10mm two-hole spacer bars. To make your own, glue the four spacers together as shown. Use two head pins to align the spacers and keep the holes free of glue.

4a On one end, string a 4mm bicone, a crimp bead, a 4mm bicone, and a lobster claw clasp. Go back through the beads just strung and tighten the wire. Repeat on the other end, substituting a soldered jump ring for the clasp. Check the fit, and add or remove beads from each end if necessary.

b Place a crimp cover over each crimp bead on the ends of the two bottom strands and close them gently with chainnose pliers.

5 **dangle:** Cut a 3-in. (7.6cm) piece of wire. String a briolette and make a set of wraps as in a top-drilled bead (Basics). Make the first half of a wrapped loop (Basics) above the wraps. Make a total of four briolette units.

6 Cut four pieces of chain to the following lengths: 1 in. (2.5cm), 1¼ in. (3.2cm), 1½ in. (3.8cm), and 1¾ in. (4.4cm). Attach a briolette unit to each chain. Complete the wraps.

7 Cut a 3-in. (7.6cm) piece of wire. Make the first half of a wrapped loop on one end. Attach each of the chains and complete the wraps. String a 4mm pearl, a 6mm bicone crystal, and a 4mm pearl. Make a wrapped loop above the top bead.

8 Open a jump ring (Basics). Attach the dangle to the fourth hole of the four-hole spacer bar. Close the jump ring.

1 **earrings** • Cut a 3-in. (7.6cm) piece of wire. String a briolette and make a set of wraps above it (Basics). Make the first half of a wrapped loop (Basics) above the wraps.

Cut a 1-in. (2.5cm) piece of chain. Attach the briolette unit to the chain and complete the wraps.

2 Cut a 2-in. (5cm) piece of wire. Make a wrapped loop on one end. String a 5mm pearl and make the first half of a wrapped loop.

Attach the chain and complete the wraps.

3 Open the loop of an earring wire. Attach the dangle. Close the loop. Make a second earring to match the first.

SUPPLY LIST

necklace
- **4** 8 x 10mm briolettes
- **18** 4mm bicone crystals
- 6mm bicone crystal
- **8** 5mm pearls
- **6** 4mm pearls
- 9g 11º seed beads in assorted colors and finishes
- flexible beading wire, .014 or .015
- four-hole spacer bar

- **4** two-hole spacer bars
- jump ring
- **6** crimp beads
- **4** crimp covers
- lobster claw clasp and soldered jump ring
- 15 in. (38cm) 24-gauge half-hard wire
- 5½ in. (14cm) chain, 2–3mm links
- chainnose pliers
- roundnose pliers
- diagonal wire cutters
- crimping pliers (optional)

earrings
- **2** 8 x 10mm briolettes
- **2** 5mm pearls
- 10 in. (25cm) 24-gauge half-hard wire
- 2½ in. (6.4cm) chain, 2–3mm links
- pair of earring wires
- chainnose pliers
- roundnose pliers
- diagonal wire cutters

Get multiple styles
from one extra-long
wood necklace

by Jane Konkel

A shapely necklace strung
with a variety of black and white
wood beads is a beautiful
addition to a turtleneck. The
necklace's versatile length
provides a variety of wardrobe
options. Wear it long, knot it, or
loop it twice over your head
for double-strand appeal.
Wire-caged earrings
provide a contemporary,
captivating accent.

Woodn't it be lovely

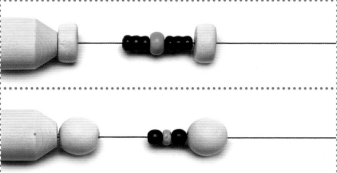

1 necklace • Determine the finished length of your necklace. (This one is 52 in./1.3m.) Add 6 in. (15cm) and cut a piece of beading wire to that length. Center a white 15mm round bead, a barrel bead, and a wheel bead on the wire.

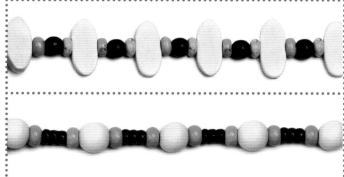

2 a On one end, string a tube bead, a 10mm rondelle, a tube, and a wheel. Repeat this pattern for one quarter of the necklace length. End with a wheel.

b On the other end, string a black round bead, a 6mm rondelle, a black round, and a white 15mm round. Repeat this pattern for one quarter of the necklace length. End with a 15mm round.

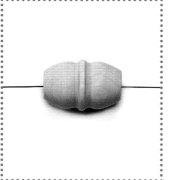

3 On each end, string a barrel bead.

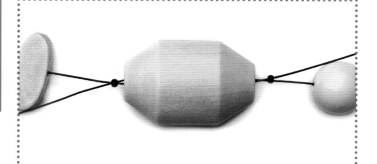

4 a On one end, string a flat oval bead, a 6mm rondelle, a black round, and a 6mm rondelle. Repeat this pattern for one quarter of the necklace length. End with a flat oval.

b On the other end, string a white 12mm round bead, a 10mm rondelle, a tube, and a 10mm rondelle. Repeat this pattern for one quarter of the necklace length. End with a 12mm round.

EDITOR'S TIP

Make sure each pattern section is one quarter of the necklace's length. Separate each section with a large bead.

5 On each end, string a crimp bead. String each end through a barrel and the adjacent crimp bead. Tighten the wires. Check the fit, and add or remove beads from each end if necessary. Crimp the crimp beads (Basics, p. 6) and trim the excess wire.

1 **earrings** • Cut a 10-in. (25cm) piece of black wire. Bend the wire to mark the midpoint. On each end, make a loop and roll the wire, forming a coil. Stop at the midpoint.

2 **a** Twist one coil upside down, forming an S shape.

b Use roundnose pliers to gently push the center of each coil out, forming two cones.

3 On a decorative head pin, string a 6mm rondelle, the center loop of one side of the cone, and a 12mm round bead. Bend the other cone over the round bead and string the cone. String a 6mm rondelle. Make a wrapped loop (Basics) above the rondelle.

4 Cut a 2-in. (5cm) piece of sterling silver wire. Make the first half of a wrapped loop on one end. Attach the bead unit and complete the wraps.

5 String a 10mm rondelle. Make a wrapped loop above the bead.

6 Open an earring wire and attach the dangle. Close the wire. Make a second earring to match the first.

SUPPLY LIST

necklace
white wood beads, 16-in. (41cm) strand each:
• 15mm round beads
• 15mm wheel beads
• 12mm round beads
• 8 x 18mm flat oval beads
• **4** 20 x 30mm barrel beads, in two shapes

black wood beads, 16-in. (41cm) strand each:
• 6 x 10mm tube beads
• 6mm round beads
gemstones, 16-in. (41cm) strand each:
• 10mm rondelles
• 6mm rondelles
• black flexible beading wire, .014 or .015
• **2** gunmetal crimp beads
• chainnose or crimping pliers
• diagonal wire cutters

earrings
• **2** 12mm white wood round beads
• **2** 10mm gemstone rondelles
• **4** 6mm gemstone rondelles
• 20 in. (51cm) 22-gauge black wire
• 4 in. (10cm) 24-gauge sterling silver half-hard wire
• **2** 2-in. (5cm) decorative head pins
• pair of earring wires
• chainnose pliers
• roundnose pliers
• diagonal wire cutters

Your jewelry might be wooden, but your personality isn't. Make a statement with this asymmetrical necklace. Smooth wood beads contrast with free-form gemstone chips and meet in a handmade toggle clasp worn off center. A turtleneck is the ideal backdrop to showcase this dynamic jewelry.

Side ways

Combine wood beads, gemstone chips, and a focal clasp in a multistrand necklace

by Paulette Biedenbender

1 necklace • Determine the finished length of your necklace. (This one is 31½ in./80cm.) Add 6 in. (15cm) and cut three pieces of beading wire to that length.

Over all three wires, string four 4mm round beads, the loop half of a clasp, three 4mm rounds, an oval bead, a 4mm round, a crimp bead, and a 4mm round. Move the beads towards one end of the wires, with the round beads closest to the short end.

2 With the short end of all three wires, go back through: oval bead, 4mm round, crimp bead, 4mm round. Tighten the wires and crimp the crimp bead (Basics, p. 6). Trim the excess wire. If desired, close a crimp cover over the crimp bead.

3 Separate the wires. On the top wire, string four 11º seed beads and two chips. On the middle wire, string three 11ºs and two chips. On the bottom wire, string two 11ºs and two chips.

4 On each wire, string a twisted-barrel wood bead and a chip, repeating for 7 in. (18cm).

EDITOR'S TIP For a more traditional look, wear the necklace with the toggle clasp front and center.

5 On each wire, string an oval and a chip, repeating for approximately 6 in. (15cm).

6 On each wire, string three chips and an 8mm round bead. String chips and an 8mm round, increasing the number of chips in each section by two to four, until the strand is within 5 in. (13cm) of the desired length. End with chips.

7 On the top wire, string four 11ºs. On the middle wire, string three 11ºs. On the bottom wire, string two 11ºs.

8 Over all three wires, string: five 4mm rounds, crimp bead, 4mm round, bar half of the clasp, wood spacer, 4mm round. Skipping the last 4mm round, go back through the beads just strung. Tighten the wires. Check the fit, and add or remove beads if necessary. Crimp the crimp bead and trim the excess wire. If desired, close a crimp cover over the crimp bead.

1 earrings • On a head pin, string a chip, a twisted-barrel wood bead, and a chip. Make a plain loop (Basics) above the chip.

2 Open the loop (Basics) of an earring post and attach the dangle. Close the loop. Make a second earring to match the first.

Come out of your shell

by Jane Konkel

Show off a turtleneck with a cleverly designed matinee-length necklace

Perhaps you shy away from wearing jewelry with a turtleneck because it gets lost in the high collar. Let go of those reservations. This necklace is long and bold enough to hold its own. Simple hoop earrings, strung with seed beads to mimic the pendant's shape, complete the look.

1 **necklace** • Determine the finished length of your necklace. (These necklaces are 24 in./61cm.) Add 8 in. (20cm) and cut two pieces of beading wire to that length.

Over both wires, string ½ in. (1.3cm) of matte 11º seed beads, a briolette pendant, and ½ in. (1.3cm) of matte 11ºs. Center the beads.

2 Over all the wires, string a spacer, the accent bead, and a 5mm round bead.

SUPPLY LIST

necklace
• 20–25mm briolette pendant
• 12–15mm accent bead
• **9–13** 5mm round beads
• 4g matte 11º seed beads
• 4g shiny 11º seed beads
• **21–29** 4mm spacers
• flexible beading wire, .014 or .015
• S-hook clasp and **2** soldered jump rings
• **2** crimp beads
• chainnose pliers
• diagonal wire cutters
• crimping pliers (optional)

earrings
• **2** 5mm round beads
• 2g matte 11º seed beads
• 2g shiny 11º seed beads
• **10** 4mm spacers
• 32 in. (81cm) 26-gauge half-hard wire
• pair of earring wires
• chainnose pliers
• roundnose pliers
• diagonal wire cutters

3 On each side of one wire, string ½ in. (1.3cm) of matte 11ºs, a spacer, 1¼ in. (3.2cm) of matte 11ºs, and a 5mm round. Repeat until the strand is within 2 in. (5cm) of the desired length.

4 On each side of the remaining wire, string 1¼ in. (3.2cm) of shiny 11ºs, a spacer, ½ in. (1.3cm) of shiny 11ºs, and the 5mm round from the first strand. Repeat until the strand is within 2 in. (5cm) of the desired length.

5 On each side, over both wires, string a spacer, a crimp bead, a spacer, and a soldered jump ring. Go back through the beads just strung and tighten the wires. Check the fit, and add or remove beads if necessary. Crimp the crimp beads (Basics, p. 6) and trim the excess wire. Attach an S-hook clasp to one of the jump rings. Close half of the clasp with chainnose pliers.

1 **earrings** • Cut two 8-in. (20cm) pieces of 26-gauge wire. Center a round bead on both wires.

2 On each side of one wire, string ½ in. (1.3cm) of matte 11º seed beads and a spacer. On each side of the remaining wire, string 1 in. (2.5cm) of shiny 11ºs and a spacer.

3 On each side of the wire with matte 11ºs, string 1 in. (2.5cm) of matte 11ºs. On each side of the wire with shiny 11ºs, string ½ in. (1.3cm) of shiny 11ºs. Form the wires into a drop shape and string a spacer over all the wires.

4 With all the wires, make a wrapped loop (Basics) above the spacer.

5 Open the loop (Basics) of an earring wire. Attach the dangle and close the loop. Make a second earring to match the first.

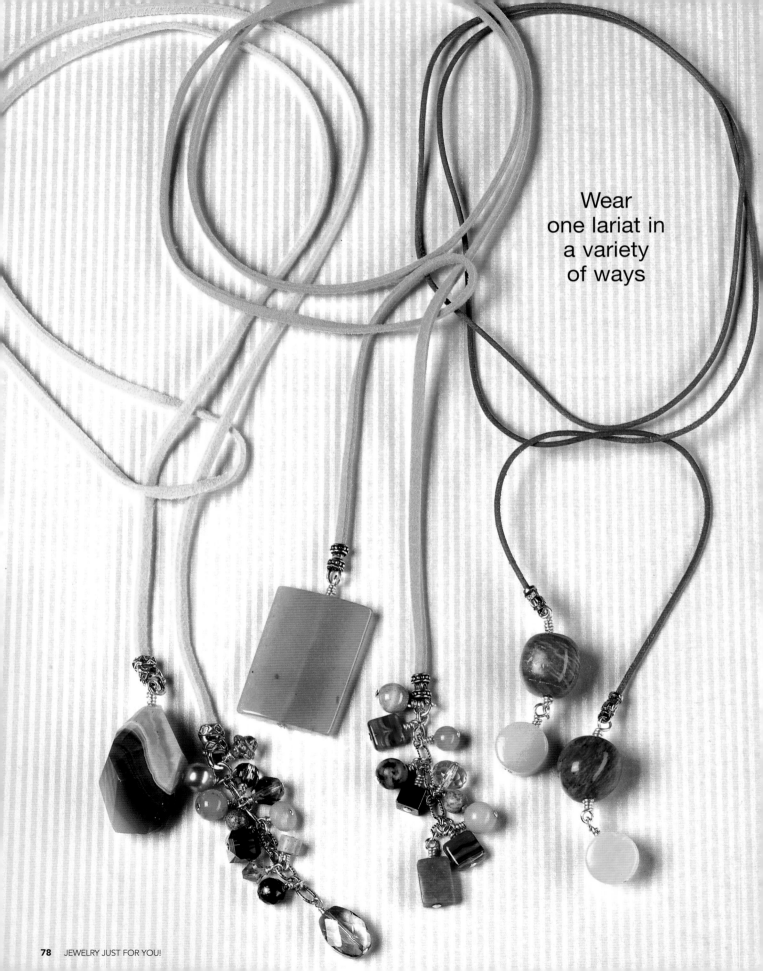

Wear
one lariat in
a variety
of ways

Wraparound style

by Deb Huber

Knotted or casually looped around your neck, a lariat is a versatile accessory for a turtleneck. You can whip up a suede or leather version in less than half an hour using a handful of assorted beads. For earrings, shape wire into large rectangles — a variation on traditional hoops.

EDITOR'S TIP
To suit your face shape, change the size of the earrings. For very large earrings, use 20-gauge half-hard wire.

1 leather lariat • Cut a 1-yd. (.9m) piece of leather cord. On each end, apply glue and attach a crimp end. Flatten the crimp portion of each crimp end with chainnose pliers (Basics, p. 6). Allow the glue to dry.

2 String a 10–14mm bead on a head pin. Make the first half of a wrapped loop (Basics) above the bead.

3 Cut a 3-in. (7.6cm) piece of wire. Make the first half of a wrapped loop at one end. String a 15–18mm bead and make the first half of a wrapped loop above the bead.

4 Attach the 10–14mm bead unit to a loop of the 15–18mm bead unit. Attach the dangle to the loop of a crimp end. Complete the wraps. Repeat steps 2–4 on the other end.

1 **suede lariat** • Cut a 1-yd. (.9m) piece of suede cord. On each end, attach a crimp end as in step 1 of the leather-lariat instructions.

2 String a 6–15mm bead on a 1½-in. (3.8cm) head pin. Make the first half of a wrapped loop (Basics) above the bead. Make a total of seven to 15 bead units.

3 Cut a 1½-in. (3.8cm) piece of chain. Attach each bead unit to various links. Complete the wraps.

4 Open a jump ring (Basics). Attach the dangle to the loop of a crimp end. Close the jump ring. If desired, attach a bead unit to the crimp end's loop.

5 String a nugget on a 3-in. (7.6cm) head pin. Make the first half of a wrapped loop above the bead. Attach the nugget's loop to the loop of the remaining crimp end. Complete the wraps.

1 **earrings** • Cut a 9-in. (23cm) piece of wire. With chainnose pliers, make a right-angle bend 3 in. (7.6cm) from one end. String five beads and make an upward right-angle bend next to the last bead.

2 Approximately 2 in. (5cm) from each bend, make a right-angle bend to form a rectangle. Bend the short wire upward at the center.

3 Wrap the long wire around the short wire, as in completing wraps (Basics). Trim the excess wrapping wire. Make a plain loop (Basics) with the remaining wire.

4 Hammer the wire on a bench block or anvil, being careful not to break the beads.

5 Open the loop (Basics) of an earring wire. Attach the dangle and close the loop. Make a second earring the mirror image of the first.

SUPPLY LIST

leather lariat
- **2** 15–18mm beads
- **2** 10–14mm beads
- 1 yd. (.9m) 1.5–2mm leather cord
- 6 in. (15cm) 22-gauge half-hard wire
- **2** 2-in. (5cm) head pins
- **2** crimp ends
- chainnose pliers
- roundnose pliers
- diagonal wire cutters
- E6000 adhesive

suede lariat
- 25–35mm nugget
- **7–15** 6–15mm beads
- 1 yd. (.9m) 3mm suede cord
- 1½ in. (3.8cm) chain, 5–6mm links
- 3-in. (7.6cm) head pin
- **7–15** 1½-in. (3.8cm) head pins
- 5mm jump ring
- **2** crimp ends
- chainnose pliers
- roundnose pliers
- diagonal wire cutters
- E6000 adhesive

earrings
- **10** 6–8mm beads, **2** of each type
- 18 in. (46cm) 22-gauge half-hard wire
- pair of earring wires
- chainnose pliers
- roundnose pliers
- diagonal wire cutters
- ball-peen hammer
- bench block or anvil

Wear a haute house bloom

Heed the call of the tropics with a floral necklace and earrings

by Jane Konkel

You may steam up every room you enter wearing this exotic beauty. No fussy hothouse diva, this orchid pendant is polyresin coated for durability. Suspended from delicate chain, the lush flower necklace-and-earring set will thrive.

EDITOR'S TIP To vary the necklace length, adjust the chain lengths in steps 6a and 7a.

1 **necklace** • Cut one 1-in. (2.5cm) and two ½-in. (1.3cm) pieces of chain. Open a jump ring (Basics, p. 6) and attach the 1-in. (2.5cm) chain to the pendant's center loop. Close the jump ring. Use jump rings to attach each remaining chain to an adjacent loop.

2 Cut a 4-in. (10cm) piece of wire. String a drop bead. Make a set of wraps above the bead (Basics).

3 String a spacer, a 10mm bead, and a spacer. Make the first half of a wrapped loop (Basics) above the bead.

4 Attach the dangle's loop to the pendant's center chain. Complete the wraps.

5 String a round crystal on a decorative head pin. Make the first half of a wrapped loop above the crystal. Attach the loop to one chain of the pendant. Complete the wraps. Repeat with a bicone crystal.

6 **a** **middle chain:** Determine the finished length of your necklace. (This necklace is 17 in./43cm.) Cut three pairs of chain, each 3–3½ in. (7.6–8.9cm) long. Cut a 2-in. (5cm) piece of wire. Make the first half of a wrapped loop on one end. String a spacer, a 10mm, and a spacer. Make the first half of a wrapped loop on the other end. Make a total of two 10mm units.

b Attach each loop of each bead unit to one pair of chains. Complete the wraps.

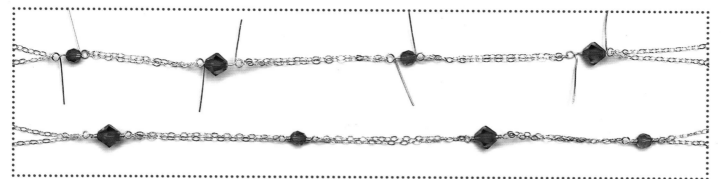

7 a top and bottom chains: Cut five pairs of chain, each 1½–2 in. (3.8–5cm) long.

b Cut a 2-in. (5cm) piece of wire. Make the first half of a wrapped loop on one end. String a crystal and make the first half of a wrapped loop on the other end. Make a total of two bicone units and two round units.

c Attach each loop of a crystal unit to one pair of chains, alternating rounds and bicones. Complete the wraps.

d Repeat steps 7a–7c to make the bottom chain, reversing the crystal pattern from the top chain.

8 a To make beaded chains for the other side of the pendant, repeat steps 6a–7d.

b Use a jump ring to attach each of the chains to the pendant's corresponding loop, as shown. To shorten the top chain slightly, trim an equal amount of chain from each side.

9 Use a jump ring to attach each of the chains to the corresponding loop of each half of a clasp. Check the fit, and trim an equal amount of chain from each end if necessary.

SUPPLY LIST

necklace
- flower pendant with four-loop finding, approx. 43 x 47mm (Fire Mountain Gems, 800-355-2137, firemountaingems.com)
- 12mm drop bead, top drilled
- **5** 10mm beads
- **9** 6mm bicone crystals
- **9** 4mm round crystals
- **10** 4mm flat spacers
- 40 in. (1m) 24-gauge half-hard wire
- 100–126 in. (2.5–3.2m) chain, 2–3mm links
- **2** 1½-in. (3.8cm) decorative head pins
- **15** 24-gauge 4mm jump rings
- multistrand clasp
- chainnose pliers
- roundnose pliers
- diagonal wire cutters

earrings
- **2** flower components with four-loop finding, approximately 10mm (Fire Mountain Gems)
- 4 ft. (1.2m) chain, 2–3mm links
- **6** 24-gauge 4mm jump rings
- pair of earring wires
- chainnose and roundnose pliers, or **2** pairs chainnose pliers
- diagonal wire cutters

1 earrings • Cut six 4-in. (10cm) pieces of chain. Open a jump ring (Basics) and attach each end of two chains and a loop of the earring component. Close the jump ring.

2 Use a jump ring to attach each end of two chains to each adjacent loop of the component.

3 Open the loop (Basics) of an earring wire and attach the top loop of the component. Close the loop. Make a second earring to match the first.

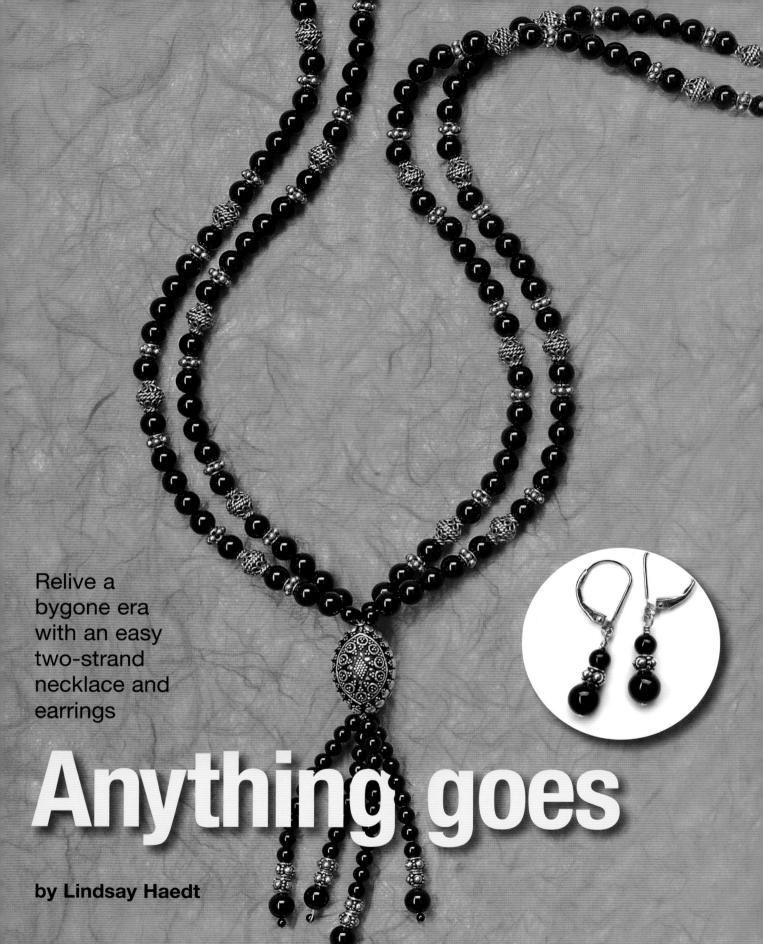

Relive a
bygone era
with an easy
two-strand
necklace and
earrings

Anything goes

by Lindsay Haedt

This long, 1920s-inspired necklace is flexible enough to fit any mood. Wear it with a strapless top or as an elegant accent to that little black dress. Shiny onyx gives this piece extra polish, but glass beads are an affordable substitute. Add a pair of simple earrings, and you can Charleston the night away.

1 **necklace** • Determine the finished length of each strand of your necklace, including the fringe. (The short strands of this necklace are 13½ in./34.3cm.) Add 6 in. (15cm) and cut two pieces of beading wire to that length. Cut two more pieces, each 1 in. (2.5cm) longer than the first two.

On one wire, string: 5mm spacer, crimp bead, 5mm spacer, 6mm round bead, 2mm round bead. Go back through the beads, skipping the 2mm. Tighten the wire and crimp the crimp bead (Basics, p. 6). Trim the excess wire. Repeat on the remaining wires.

2 On each strand, string eight to 11 4mm rounds.

4 On each strand, string: 6mm spacer, 6mm round, accent bead, 6mm round, 6mm spacer, four 6mm rounds. Repeat until the strands are within 1½ in. (3.8cm) of the desired length. End with a 6mm round.

3 String the focal bead over all four strands. On the long strands, string a 4mm and four 6mm rounds. On the short strands, string a 4mm and two 6mm rounds.

5 On each end of each strand, string: 5mm spacer, crimp bead, 5mm spacer, 4mm, the corresponding loop of half of a clasp. Go back through the beads just strung. Tighten the wires and check the fit. Add or remove beads from each end, if necessary. Crimp the crimp beads and trim the excess wire.

SUPPLY LIST

necklace
- 22mm focal bead
- **2** 16-in. (41cm) strands 6mm round beads
- **40–52** 4mm round beads
- **4** 2mm round beads
- **20–30** 8mm accent beads
- **40–50** 6mm spacers
- **16** 5mm spacers
- flexible beading wire, .014 or .015
- **8** crimp beads
- two-strand clasp

- chainnose or crimping pliers
- diagonal wire cutters

earrings
- **2** 6mm round beads
- **2** 4mm round beads
- **2** 5mm spacers
- **2** 1½-in. (3.8cm) head pins
- pair of lever-back earring wires
- chainnose pliers
- roundnose pliers
- diagonal wire cutters

1 **earrings** • String a 6mm round bead, a 5mm spacer, and a 4mm round bead on a head pin. Make a wrapped loop (Basics) above the top bead.

2 Open the loop (Basics) of an earring wire and attach the dangle. Close the loop. Make a second earring to match the first.

Stocky options

Invest in a feature-flattering choker and earrings • by Jane Konkel

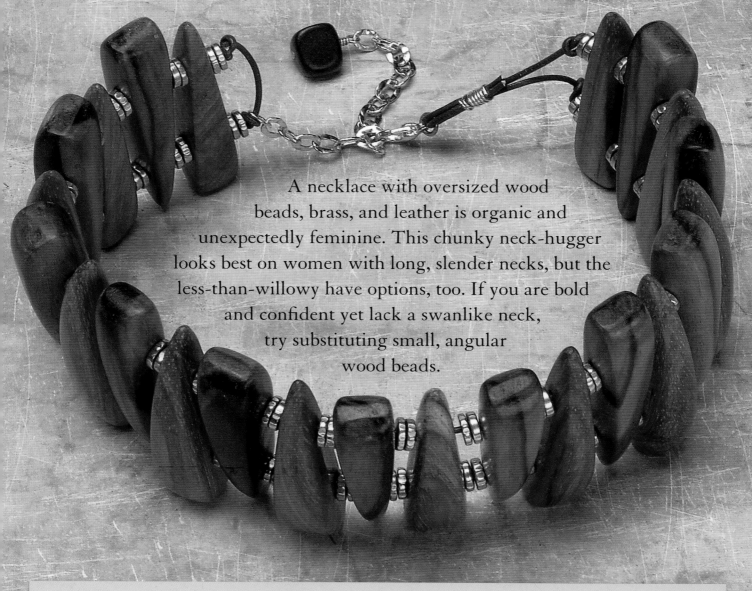

A necklace with oversized wood beads, brass, and leather is organic and unexpectedly feminine. This chunky neck-hugger looks best on women with long, slender necks, but the less-than-willowy have options, too. If you are bold and confident yet lack a swanlike neck, try substituting small, angular wood beads.

SUPPLY LIST

necklace
- **2** 8-in. (20cm) strands 15 x 54mm beads: bayong wood and tiger ebony wood, double drilled (Beads and Pieces, 707-765-2890, beadsandpieces.com)
- 10mm wood bead
- 16-in. (41cm) strand 6mm flat spacers
- 39–45 in. (1–1.1m) 1mm leather cord
- 4 in. (10cm) 24-gauge half-hard wire
- 1½-in. (3.8cm) head pin
- 4 in. (10cm) chain, 5–6mm links
- lobster claw clasp with 5mm soldered jump ring
- chainnose pliers
- diagonal wire cutters

earrings
- **4** 10mm wood beads
- **8** 6mm flat spacers
- 10 in. (25cm) 1mm leather cord
- 6 in. (15cm) 24-gauge half-hard wire
- pair of earring wires
- chainnose pliers
- diagonal wire cutters

1 **necklace** • Determine the finished length of your choker. (This one is 15½ in./39.4cm.) Double that measurement, add 8 in. (20cm), and cut a piece of leather cord to that length. Tie a knot at the center of the cord, and string two spacers. String the narrow end of a wood bead.

2 String an end link of a 4-in. (10cm) piece of chain. Approximately 1 in. (2.5cm) from the first knot, tie a knot. String two spacers and the bottom hole (the wide end) of the wood bead.

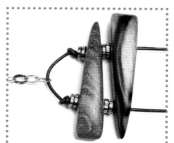

3 On each end, string two spacers. String a wood bead, narrow end down. Repeat, alternating the position of the wood beads, until the necklace is within 2 in. (5cm) of the desired length. End with two spacers.

4 On each end, tie a knot next to the last spacer. Over both ends, string a lobster claw clasp and position it 1½ in. (3.8cm) from the knots.

5 Fold the cord to form a loop. Wrap 24-gauge wire securely around the gathered cords, and tuck the ends under the wraps. Use pliers to crimp the wire. Trim the excess cord and wire.

6 String a 10mm bead on a head pin. Make the first half of a wrapped loop (Basics, p. 6) above the bead. Attach the loop to the end link of chain and complete the wraps.

EDITOR'S TIP
For a lighter look, string two or three additional spacers between the wood beads.

1 **earrings** • Cut a 5-in. (13cm) piece of leather cord. Tie a knot on one end. String a spacer, a wood bead, and a spacer above the knot.

2 Cut a 3-in. (7.6cm) piece of 24-gauge wire. Fold the cord. Leaving a small loop, wrap the wire securely around the gathered cord. Tuck and crimp the wire as in step 5 of the necklace.

3 String a spacer, a wood bead, and a spacer. Tie a knot approximately 2¼ in. (5.7cm) from the end of the wraps. Trim the excess cord.

4 Open an earring wire and attach the dangle. Close the wire. Make a second earring the mirror image of the first.

With a strapless dress, try a minimalist necklace to complete your perfect look. Keep the necklace simple — petite bead clusters on a strand of metallic seed beads are pretty and unfussy.

A continuous silver strand shines against a strapless background

Silver slivers

by Naomi Fujimoto

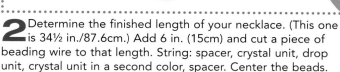

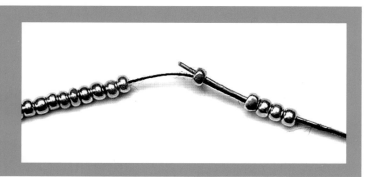

1 String a drop bead on a head pin. Make a 3mm wrapped loop (Basics, p. 6) above the bead. Make 16–20 drop units. String a bicone crystal on a head pin. Make a 3mm wrapped loop above the bead. Make 32–40 crystal units in two colors.

2 Determine the finished length of your necklace. (This one is 34½ in./87.6cm.) Add 6 in. (15cm) and cut a piece of beading wire to that length. String: spacer, crystal unit, drop unit, crystal unit in a second color, spacer. Center the beads.

3 On each end, string 1 in. (2.5cm) of 13º seed beads, an accent bead, and 1 in. (2.5cm) of 13ºs.

4 **a** On each end, string: spacer, 1 in. (2.5cm) of 13ºs, crystal unit, drop unit, crystal unit in a second color.
   b On each end, string an accent bead and 1 in. (2.5cm) of 13ºs. Repeat the patterns in steps 4a and 4b until the necklace is within 2 in. (5cm) of the desired length. End with a spacer or an accent bead.

5 On each end, string 1 in. (2.5cm) of 13ºs and a spacer. On one end, string a crimp bead. (If desired, also string a trio of bead units.) With the other end, go through the crimp bead and spacer. Tighten the wires. Check the fit, and add or remove beads from each end if necessary. Crimp the crimp bead (Basics) and trim the excess wire.

SUPPLY LIST

- 15-in. (38cm) strand 6 x 9mm faceted drops, vertically drilled
- **32–40** 4mm bicone crystals in two colors
- **16–20** 2–3mm accent beads
- hank 13º seed beads
- **18–22** 3–3.5mm round spacers
- flexible beading wire, .014 or .015
- **48–60** 1½-in. (3.8cm) 24- or 26-gauge head pins
- crimp bead
- chainnose pliers
- roundnose pliers
- diagonal wire cutters
- crimping pliers (optional)

EDITOR'S TIPS

- For faster stringing, transfer seed beads directly from the hank to the flexible beading wire, as shown.

- In the necklace, make the wrapped loop of each bead unit large enough to pass over the seed beads but not over the round spacers. Mark one jaw of your roundnose pliers with a permanent marker so you'll be able to make consistently sized loops. (You can remove the mark later with rubbing alcohol.)

Wardrobe wonder

Simple adjustments let crystals flatter any neckline • by Kathie Scrimgeour

A circle of prism crystals is the start of a quartet of necklaces that will complement every neckline in your wardrobe. Leave the prisms unadorned for a round neckline. Add graduated dangles for a V-neck. Try a wider and less pointed line of dangles to flatter a strapless look. Or, lengthen the original strand of prisms with jump rings to make a turtleneck-friendly necklace. Easy drop earrings finish any of the looks.

Round

Strapless

V-neck

Turtleneck

SUPPLY LIST

round necklace
- **20–22** 14mm prism crystals (Jewelry Supply Inc., 916-780-9610, jewelrysupply.com)
- 6mm bicone crystal
- 2-in. (5cm) head pin
- **21–23** 5mm inside diameter jump rings
- lobster claw clasp
- 2 in. (5cm) cable chain for extender, 3–4mm links
- chainnose pliers
- roundnose pliers
- diagonal wire cutters

V-neck necklace
- **22–24** 14mm prism crystals (Jewelry Supply Inc.)
- **3** 11 x 5.5mm drop crystals (Jewelry Supply Inc.)
- **5** 8mm bicone crystals

- **7** 6mm bicone crystals
- **12** 6mm round crystals
- 12 in. (30cm) 24-gauge half-hard wire
- **3** 2-in. (5cm) head pins
- **30–32** 5mm inside diameter jump rings
- lobster claw clasp
- 2 in. (5cm) cable chain for extender, 3–4mm links
- chainnose pliers
- roundnose pliers
- diagonal wire cutters

strapless necklace
- **22–24** 14mm prism crystals (Jewelry Supply Inc.)
- **5** 11 x 5.5mm drop crystals (Jewelry Supply Inc.)
- **9** 8mm bicone crystals
- **7** 6mm bicone crystals
- **10** 6mm round crystals

- 16 in. (41cm) 24-gauge half-hard wire
- **5** 2-in. (5cm) head pins
- **36–38** 5mm inside diameter jump rings
- lobster claw clasp
- 2 in. (5cm) cable chain for extender, 3–4mm links
- chainnose pliers
- roundnose pliers
- diagonal wire cutters

turtleneck necklace
- **20–22** 14mm prism crystals (Jewelry Supply Inc.)
- 6mm bicone crystal
- 2-in. (5cm) head pin
- **65–68** 8mm inside diameter jump rings
- lobster claw clasp
- chainnose pliers
- roundnose pliers

earrings
- **2** 14mm prism crystals (Jewelry Supply Inc.)
- **2** 8mm bicone crystals
- **2** 6mm bicone crystals
- 4 in. (10cm) 24-gauge half-hard wire
- **2** 5mm inside diameter jump rings
- pair of earring wires
- chainnose pliers
- roundnose pliers
- diagonal wire cutters

ALL SHAPES neckline

Round

1 **round necklace •** Open a jump ring (Basics, p. 6). Attach two prism crystals. Close the jump ring. Continue linking prisms and jump rings until the strand has an even number of prisms and is within 1 in. (2.5cm) of the desired length. (This one is 14 in./36cm.)

2 Open a jump ring. Attach a lobster claw clasp and the end prism. Close the jump ring. Repeat on the other end, substituting a 2-in. (5cm) chain for the clasp.

3 String a 6mm bicone crystal on a head pin. Make the first half of a wrapped loop (Basics). Attach the crystal unit to the end of the chain. Complete the wraps.

1 V-neck necklace •

a Make the round necklace.

b Cut a 3-in. (7.6cm) piece of wire. Make a plain loop on one end. String two 6mm bicone crystals and two round crystals. Make a plain loop.

c Cut a 3-in. (7.6cm) piece of wire. Make a plain loop (Basics) on one end. String two round crystals, two 6mm bicone crystals, and an 8mm bicone crystal. Make a plain loop.

3
Cut a 3-in. (7.6cm) piece of wire. Make a plain loop on one end. Open the loop and string a prism crystal. Close the loop.

4
String two round crystals and an 8mm bicone. Make a plain loop.

Repeat steps 3 and 4 to make a second prism unit.

2
Open a jump ring (Basics) and attach a drop crystal and the round-crystal end of the longer dangle. Close the jump ring.

Use a jump ring to attach the bicone ends of the two crystal units.

Use a jump ring to attach the dangle to the center jump ring of the prism strand.

5
Use a jump ring to attach a drop crystal to the end of a prism unit. Repeat on the second prism unit.

Use a jump ring to attach a prism dangle next to the center dangle. Repeat on the other side.

V-neck

6
On a 2-in. (5cm) head pin, string an 8mm bicone, a 6mm bicone, and two round crystals. Make a plain loop. Repeat to make a second dangle.

7
Use a jump ring to attach a dangle next to the prism dangle. Repeat on the other side.

Strapless

1 **strapless necklace •**
Make the round necklace. Make the dangle as in step 1c of the V-neck necklace and attach a drop crystal as in step 2. Attach the dangle to the center of the necklace. Continue with steps 3–7 of the V-neck necklace.

Cut a 2-in. (5cm) piece of wire. Make a plain loop on one end. String an 8mm bicone crystal. Make a plain loop. Repeat to make a second crystal unit.

2 Open a jump ring and attach a drop crystal to a crystal unit. Close the jump ring. Use a jump ring to attach the dangle next to the previous dangle. Repeat on the other side.

3 On a head pin, string an 8mm bicone and a 6mm bicone. Make a plain loop. Repeat to make a second dangle.

4 Open a jump ring and attach a dangle next to the previous dangle. Repeat on the other side.

Turtleneck

DESIGN GUIDELINE
To make longer earrings, use a jump ring to attach a drop crystal to the remaining hole of the prism crystal.

turtleneck necklace • Make the round necklace, attaching three jump rings between the prism crystals instead of one. (With the additional jump rings, this necklace is 21 in./53cm, so you can omit the extender.)

1 **earrings** • Cut a 2-in. (5cm) piece of wire. Make a plain loop (Basics) on one end. String an 8mm bicone crystal and a 6mm bicone crystal. Make a plain loop.

2 Open a jump ring (Basics) and attach a prism crystal and the bottom loop. Close the jump ring.

Open the loop (Basics) of an earring wire and attach the dangle. Close the loop. Make a second earring to match the first.

CONTRIBUTORS

Rupa Balachandar is passionate about all things gem and jewelry related and is a regular contributor to *BeadStyle* magazine. She enjoys creating fashionable, affordable, and easy-to-make jewelry. For a wide selection of unique pendants and beads, visit her Web site, rupab.com, or e-mail her at info@rupab.com.

Formerly with *BeadStyle* magazine, Paulette Biedenbender now owns the store Bead Needs in Hales Corners, Wis. Contact her at 414-529-5211 or visit her Web site, beadneedsllc.com.

Contact Gloria Farver at rfarver@wi.rr.com.

Naomi Fujimoto is Senior Editor of *BeadStyle* magazine and the author of *Cool Jewels: Beading Projects for Teens*. Visit her blog at cooljewelsnaomi.blogspot.com or contact her in care of *BeadStyle*.

Jennifer Gorski creates jewelry from her home in the Rocky Mountains of Colorado. Jewelry inspirations often come to her in the middle of the night while she is sleeping. Contact Jennifer at djgorski@comcast.net.

Lindsay Haedt is Editorial Associate of *BeadStyle*. Contact her through the magazine.

Contact Deb Huber via e-mail at dlhuber@comcast.net, or visit clever-treasures.com.

Cathy Jakicic is Editor of *BeadStyle*. Contact her through the magazine.

Jane Konkel is Associate Editor of *BeadStyle* and also indulges her crafty side as a contributor to *Make it Mine* magazine. Contact her in care of *BeadStyle*.

Kim Lucas has been creating beaded jewelry as a hobby for several years. Her designs have previously appeared in *BeadStyle* magazine. Contact her at klucas123@hotmail.com.

Juli Martin is a full-time college student at Oberlin College in Oberlin, Ohio. Contact her at julridesigns@gmail.com or through her online shop, julridesigns.etsy.com.

Contact Kerry Melson at rust567@aol.com, or visit her Web site, theresaspromise.com.

Denaé Oglesby is a jewelry artist whose designs feature precious metal clay, as well as natural semi-precious and precious gemstones. She lives in Knoxville, Tenn., and can be contacted via e-mail at oglesbyd@comcast.net.

Contact Molli Schultz at fragile_bymollischultz@yahoo.com.

Kathie Scrimgeour has been a jewelry designer for over four years. Her work has been published in *BeadStyle* and online in the *Bead Bugle*. Contact her via e-mail at kjscrim@yahoo.com.

Trained in jewelry design at the Fashion Institute of Technology in New York, Sara Strauss can be contacted her via e-mail at bluestaro@hotmail.com. Visit her Web site, sgsjewelry.com, to see her work.

BEAD WITH THE BEAUTY OF BIRTHSTONES

Easy Birthstone Jewelry

38 Exciting Projects
Personalized designs
for everyone
you know –
and you, too!

Bead Style BOOKS

This collection of 38 projects is divided into twelve sections (one for each month), each featuring a description of the traditional and alternate birthstones for that month and three projects. There is also a short section featuring mothers' sets and other jewelry that combines birthstone varieties. The projects will include necklaces, bracelets, earrings and more, and can be made with a few basic techniques. 112 pages.

62557 • $21.95

String or stitch something stunning with these books

Beading Inspiration
How to use COLOR in jewelry design

Bead Style

Packed with new and traditional approaches to designing with color that will expand any beader's current palette as well as increase creative confidence. Explores using nature, the color wheel, decorative art, and fabric for color inspiration. 96 pages.
62465 • $19.95

Seed Bead Stitching
BEAD
Creative Variations on Traditional Techniques

Beth Stone

This book covers the basic beadweaving stitches, but will also show readers alternate stitches and new possibilities. Readers will learn to create a variety of projects, including necklaces, pendants, bracelets, and rings. 96 pages.
62526 • $19.95

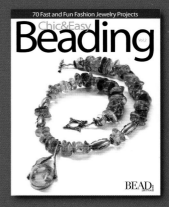

70 Fast and Fun Fashion Jewelry Projects
Chic&Easy Beading vol.2
BEAD

Compiled from the pages of *Chic&Easy*, *Bead&Button*, and *BeadStyle*, this book showcases 70 fabulous jewelry projects that can be made in a flash with only a few techniques. An illustrated basics section includes all the instructions beginners need to get started. 144 pages.
62253 • $21.95

Available at your favorite bead or craft store!
Or order direct at www.BeadAndCraftBooks.com
Call 1-800-533-6644 Mon-Fri, 8:30am-5:00pm Central Time.
Outside the U.S. and Canada, call 262-796-8776 x661.

BKS-BDB-6261BRH

XBB